*Writing History*

# WRITING HISTORY

SHERMAN KENT

YALE UNIVERSITY

1941   F. S. CROFTS & CO.   New York

PE 1478
.K4

*For*
*Elizabeth Thacher Kent*

# Preface

A good many of our universities insist that their undergraduates who major in history cap the major with an essay. Departments of history generally consider it a serious piece of research and writing; one which demands, in his junior and senior years, a good part of the student's time, his patience, ingenuity, and his sense of artistry. Nearly everyone who begins such a job begins at scratch. Not only does he not know what he's going to write about and how, but very frequently he doesn't know why. Aside from the college rule that says he must, he can't understand the virtue of discovering and writing up some historical truth when others who are paid for such things would do it better. In the preliminary skirmishes his director or supervisor or tutor takes something of a beating.

Nor are the preliminary skirmishes the only ones. Convinced that there is no other way around, the student's next questions are generally: "How long does it have to be? What shall I write about? Do you have to footnote every statement you make?" When the topic is found and research moves on there are different questions but no abatement in number. Answering them, while one of the director's most tedious duties, is also one of his most important. Well indeed does he remember last year's most incorrigible who began his essay only under threats of violence, and who ended with seventy-five pages on Geronimo which were published that summer. The director realizes that his best teaching is done when he is explaining for the thousandth time how you pursue a topic through a library, how you take notes on cards, why you bother to keep track of the places your information comes from, how you cite books and manuscripts in your footnotes, what you put in your bibliographical note, and how you put it there. Not that this book will relieve him of all explaining. What I hope is that it will make the more mechanical kinds of instruction unnecessary.

Graduate students very often need more advice and more detailed advice than essay-writing seniors. For their benefit I have amplified Chapter VI ("Style and Usage") beyond normal undergraduate needs, and included the appendix on how to make an index.

In putting such a book together I have tried to avoid riding my own hobby horses. This means that I have called upon friends and colleagues to such an extent that the book might better be theirs. But since someone must be responsible for its shortcomings, I gladly claim them.

For anything good I want to thank John Allison, John Andrews, Gould Coleman, Archibald Foord, Helen Frost, John Gee, Basil Henning, Beecher Hogan, Beth Kent, William Kip, Thomas Mendenhall, Henry Rowell, Dorothy Schade and Richard Schermerhorn. I want to thank the editors of the University of Chicago Press for their kind permission to use passages from § 138 and § 150 of their admirable *Manual of Style*. Especially do I want to thank Bertha Josephson for giving me an advance glimpse of part of the style book she has in preparation, and for allowing me to use a few of her examples. Then I want to thank Dorothy Gray, Leonard Labaree, and Hartley Simpson for their help on the style chapter and the appendix. I shouldn't call it help: these pages might better bear their signatures. Then I want to thank Dixon Ryan Fox, the editor of this series, for his manifold kindnesses. And last, I want to say that Wallace Notestein and Hajo Holborn are the people to whom I am most grateful. Their willingness to squander time over typescripts and typescripts and their happy eagerness to encourage and exhort are the only reasons that this manuscript is in print and not ashes.

S. K.

# Contents

*Writing History*

# CHAPTER I

# Why History

It is just as well for us that the past does not die. It is just as well that despite the altruistic note of one of our adages we are not able to let bygones be bygones. It is our good fortune that we remember, and that we have perfected techniques to prop naked memory with the written record and to make it more durable and accurate. Our custom of taking records and preserving them is the main barrier that separates us from the scatter-brained races of monkey. For it is this extension of memory that permits us to draw upon experience and which allows us to establish a common pool of wisdom. Apart from the power to create, this power to store up creations and observations is man's most significant advantage over other creatures. Knowledge of things said and done—notice the past tense—is a knowledge which not merely sees us through the trivial decisions of the moment, but also stands by in the far more important times of personal or public crisis. And "knowledge of things said and done" is Carl Becker's all-inclusive definition of history.[1]

/ Whether we like it or not, we live in the middle of history. We consume as much history as air. The prudent man uses it to tell him not to eat fish in July, because last July he got sick from eating fish. The judge uses it to decide how serious a man's offense is—"What penalty have others suffered for a similar

1. *Everyman His Own Historian* (N.Y., 1935), pp. 233-255.

I

crime?" he asks himself. The doctor uses it in the diagnosis of symptoms; the businessman and the statesman use it when they reflect upon the smart move or the socially expedient move. /

Consider the passage of any piece of legislation; consider for example the passage of our own Social Security bill. This law like practically all legislation was drafted and presented, debated and amended; it was signed. In each step of its confection, the men of one opinion or another flung themselves against the problems it brought forth. There was controversy. A large part of the controversy was conducted on the basis of remembered past experience. It is impossible to believe that some Congressman did not cite Europe's earlier experiments with social security, and that another did not counter with a pointed reference to Rome's bread and circuses. It is likely that debate around the questions of finance and the prospects of state help produced a sketchy financial history of the United States, and a slim world history of social legislation. It is likely that during the debate some of the argument at least departed so far from the subject itself that it bore merely upon the validity or invalidity of the various historical analogies which both parties advanced. Knowledge of things said and done—*history*—was a crucial if not decisive weapon, and when social security (or any other piece of big legislation for that matter) rides into American life argument from historical analogy supplies the whip. What history was to this act, it was to almost all the other acts of this and other congresses which have argued in Washington, in Paris, in London and Rome.

History is useful. Writing history accurately is an act of public service. But writing it accurately is hard—some people would say impossible.

If we adopt Carl Becker's definition, we see at once that there has been a great deal of history. So much in fact that no

owledge. A man who paints on canvas, writes poetry, or
rves stone—no matter how badly—has a deeper apprecia-
on of the technical problems of the master painters, poets,
nd sculptors than the armchair critic. And by the same token
he man who has submitted himself to the discipline of writ-
ng history takes on critical astuteness in his reading of history.
From personal knowledge of the difficulties of writing his
own, he will detect with a sharper wit the shabby or brilliant
work of another. As long as historical analogy plays a part in
the discussion of social and political and moral questions, a
sharpness for historical truth is a useful piece of mental equipment. There is still much to be said for the medieval principle
of learning from the ground up.

The last, the most serious, reason why it is worth the student's while to write his own history is that by doing so he
will come into intimate contact with the chief philosophical
assumptions behind his existence. For if his work have any
merit at all, it will have come from the systematic nature of his
research and thought.

Systematic study or higher criticism is one of the foremost
products of rationalism besides being its fundamental prop.
The rationalists are the people who hold that the mind, when
playing in the channels of right logic, can solve any problem
it can set itself; and since many of the most compelling problems which beset the rationalist are problems of society—how
to do away with poverty, disease, and war; how to promote
happiness, health, and peace—he is likely to become a liberal.
For the liberal believes that the mind, when turned upon social
dilemmas, is capable of performing a positive and helpful
social function. Now, although not all rationalists are liberals,
all real liberals at least must be rationalists. And the result is
that the intellectual milieu of our society is heavily laden with
a respect for reason and an optimistic faith in social conscience

one man, or group of men, could ever expec
all. No one in his right mind would try, for
construct all of the things which all of the m
race have said and done since they climbed ou
No one, no matter how socially important he c
job, would dream of trying to write a moment
universal history. What he would do, and what h
times done, has been to select a particular and rest
area of human doings which he considered importan
as much about it as he could, and write down his co
Such a study, because it is a picture of one restrict
phenomena, the historians call a monograph. For
reasons the making of such a study is commendable.

In the first place, to break off a significant fragment
human past and examine it closely is an act of some soci
portance. The man who feels his social obligation and
covenants to pay his way in life by historical research
tributes to society's formal store of useful memory. Often
may find that, because of his work, an important part of
world's business is conducted in a new and better way. Be
trice and Sidney Webb had this very experience. Their clo
study of English local government became the reference boo
of Lloyd George's Liberal government, and for some seven
years it was the pillar of fire out in front of the movement to
recast England's manner of living in a more decent form. On
the other hand (and this quite parenthetically) if the fragment of the past is in itself insignificant, and if the student of
history makes no effort to relate it to his own larger world,
his work is of no social importance whatever. In these circumstances the historians say it is not history, but what they
somewhat scathingly call mere antiquarianism.

In the second place, writing a history essay or monograph
—and here for the first time I speak specifically to the novice
historian—carries with it the great experience of first-hand

if it be led by the dictates of the mind. Our bill of rights and our liberal democratic tradition make free and systematic inquiry as typical of the American way as succotash and ham and eggs.

To be a little more explicit about the meaning of systematic study in the field of history, the phrase in brief means: study within a philosophical frame of fixed points, study within the barrier of carefully defined terms and consistent statement, statement which does not wind back upon and contradict itself. It means analysis which proceeds from a clean place, not from one cluttered with other men's misstatements and inept interpretations. It means the telling of a story, every important word of which is used in consonance with a previously reasoned meaning.

So much for bases; the implications are vast. Chiefly does "systematic" study imply skepticism of things taken for granted. To the serious devotee of higher criticism there are few if any constants; all things, even the most certain, demand analysis. This does not mean that the history student must necessarily prove for himself the speed of light or the pull of gravity before he mentions them, but it does urge that he question things he has long taken as equally well established. Words like progress and power and democracy and faith he must wonder about and if possible revalue in his own terms. Smaller things like dates, spellings of proper and place names, established statistics, he must challenge, pending his own confirmation. Long-sung generalizations he must inevitably question together with the accepted epigrams and catchwords from the past. He can no longer live and act on proverbs; he will have to realize that upon occasions half a loaf is worse than no bread, and looking a gift horse in the teeth is the most proper of all possible gestures.

Ernst Bernheim was one of the first to make a systematic

study of the systematic study of historical method. In his *Manual of Historical Method and Philosophy of History*,[2] he described it in four steps: (1) *Heuristik*, the gathering of historical evidence; (2) *Kritik*, the evaluating of this evidence; (3) *Auffassung*, the moment of comprehending the true meaning of the evaluated evidence; (4) *Darstellung*, the presentation of the new idea in terms of the evaluated evidence. Not that this pattern of progressive steps was new, nor even the general argument, for the method of history is closely akin to the method of science which Francis Bacon put forth in the early seventeenth century. What was new was the suggested use of the techniques of the natural sciences upon purely man-made evidence.

Historical evidence is a bulky affair. For in the broad sense it is everything there is in our world that bears the mark of man's hand. In an excellent book, which the beginner will read with enjoyment, Allan Nevins [3] divides it into two large categories: remains and records. By remains, he means such things as buildings, roads, pots, weapons, cemeteries, and the like which, without carrying any kind of written inscription, are nevertheless evidences of human thought and deed. By records, he means everything from the chiseled legend and tooled clay brick through papyrus and parchment manuscript to longhand, print, and the human voice recorded on discs of wax. It is easy to see why historical evidence is bulky, and why the historian who is using it must try to use only those portions which tell the story best. In other words it is clear that a rigorous critical attitude is absolutely essential in order to

2. Still crying for a translator. The German title is *Lehrbuch der historischen Methode und der Geschichtsphilosophie* (6th ed., Leipzig, 1908; 1st ed., 1889). There are a number of excellent books on historical method in English. See the Historical Method section of the bibliographical note of this book, pp. 110–111.

3. *The Gateway to History* (N.Y., 1938).

make any sense out of the welter and complexity of the raw materials.

Criticizing thus becomes an elemental phase of systematic historical research; and criticizing is perhaps a little more complicated than the beginner would suspect. For first of all it encompasses the desire to detect the wholly false, the fake evidence which has been deliberately planted in order to deceive. Both remains and records have been falsified for a variety of motives: the "donation" of Constantine in order to shore up the temporal claims of the papacy; Laurence Sterne's letters, and Leonardo's "Mona Lisa" for cold cash. Gaston Means let out a purely imaginary *Strange Death of President Harding* because he was a psychopathic egotist and liar; James Bryce lent his name to a bluebook full of improbable atrocity stories because he felt it his patriotic duty. The historian must have a mulish obstinacy, a refusal to be gulled; he must be incredulous of his evidence or he will trip over the deliberately falsified.

Next, his critical sense is necessary to correct evidence which has not been tampered with, but which is misleading because of its incompleteness. When the tenth-century chronicler, Richer, spoke of Hugh Capet (later chosen as first of the great line of Capetian kings) as *Dux* (the Duke), and gave the title to no one else, did he mean to set Hugh apart from the other nobles whom he lumped together as *principes* (the great men)? Was his contemporary audience so familiar with the pre-eminence of Hugh that there was no necessity to stress the point? Or was the word *Dux* an inadvertence which by no means singled its bearer out as the logical successor to the throne? Or what did the English lady mean when she wrote an American friend, "John is back after three rather uncomfortable days on Dunkirk beach"? Did she mean that John found the weather too brisk for swimming; or did she mean that John had put in three days in the maddest hell of recent human contrivance? Bernheim's *Kritik* in this sense means nothing more than a proper skepticism and a desire to get behind the surface to a real and intended meaning, which the frailties of the human power to express had obscured.

Then criticism comes into historical investigations a third way. It enters in the guise of general wisdom and intellectual balance. "Compensation to the miners of the southern bituminous coal field is below the living wage." On the face of things the statement is simple and clear: the miners are not paid enough to live on. But is this the meaning? If they can't live, then they die. Yet we know that this is not the real meaning of the sentence. We know that not many of the miners just stop eating and die. What is a living wage? How many dollars and cents per day is it? Well, living is what? Is it food, shelter, and clothing alone? Is it the mere maintenance of breath, or is it something besides? How much besides? What ought a man to expect in the way of necessities and amenities in order to make life living? Is education, for example, a luxury, or a necessity? Is it true that the widow of a one-time multimillionaire feels more poverty on five thousand a year, than a miner does on three hundred and fifty? Can five thousand dollars be called a living wage for the lady? Should it be so called?

Would the man who simply repeated the statement about the living wage without analyzing it be a historian? I would say not. Yet on the other hand to give the matter its proper critical evaluation would call forth talents which historians do not naturally possess. The questions which the concept "living wage" brings up are questions which are by no means solely historical. They are from the realms of economics, sociology, psychology, and ethics, and only the most perfectly informed man could hope to give a set of satisfactory answers. In short, criticism and the critical faculty is used here almost as a synonym for intellectual curiosity and understanding, as a synonym for mental competence.

\ There is a last way in which criticism appears in the historical process—the historian's criticism of himself. And of all, this one is the most important. Willingness to criticize his own judgments, his own conclusions in the light of what he knows or suspects of his own prejudice is the quality that separates the intellectually honest historian from the irresponsible apologist./To pause to inquire, "Am I calling Wilhelm II a rascal because his rascality is in the evidence, or am I calling him a rascal because at the moment I don't like Germans, and does my present dislike of Germans come from Hitler's Jewish policy?" and to answer with right intellectual candor is the mark of the creative critical scholar. When the evidence seems to force a single and immediate conclusion, then that is the time to worry about one's bigotry, and to do a little conscientious introspection into why this particular conclusion stands out. Was it in the material or was it in you? The command of Socrates, "know thyself," never gave richer rewards than in the world of what we've been calling systematic study.

But possibly knowing yourself more strictly belongs in Bernheim's third stage of the historical process, the step which he calls *Auffassung*, the moment of conception or comprehension. This moment is not one which is confined to research in history; it is an intimate and essential moment in all creative thought. For it is the time when the mind makes a tentative connection between any two or more phenomena that confront it. The connection is called a hypothesis. Since there will be a good deal more about hypotheses in a later chapter let us touch upon them only as they relate to the systematics of history.

It is somewhat presumptuous to generalize about good history and bad history; it is even dangerous. But the odds are that bad history results more often from errors at the *comprehension* stage than from mistakes at the earlier periods of gathering and criticizing. Often in the history of historical writing has an unplumbed prejudice or subconscious bias crippled an otherwise flawless technique of research. The best support of this statement lies mutely in the titles of whole schools of historians: the *official* historians of the third French Republic, the *national* historians of nineteenth-century Germany, the *whig* historians of Victorian England, the *patriotic* historians of the United States. The italicized words indicate that the hypotheses of these men were consciously or unconsciously tinctured by a political or personal cause and that the men themselves were blind to data which they should have seen and didn't, or which, having seen, they allowed themselves to disregard. Implied is the rather common, but nonetheless uncomplimentary accusation, that time, place, race, political conviction, economic status, social environment, and a lot of other external forces drove these historians into hypotheses which the rest of the world now recognizes as subjective. Implied also is a crueler accusation (and one which is by no means justified) that so hidebound were they that they might have composed their work without more than an uncritical glance at the records. The point is that personal bias will probably always be present at the moment of hypothesis, and the truly conscientious student of history will be waiting there to identify it, catch it, and knock it on the head before it gets woven into narrative.

The narrative is the last step in the systematic process of writing history. A last word and an important one about the story itself. Nobody expects or asks that when the historical process has spun itself into this last stage it will represent a neutrality of opinion. No one desires this any more than he desires a judge to be neutral in judging a case. The historian like the judge must reach a conclusion if he is to earn his salt.

He cannot examine the evidence on both sides and close out the case with the cloying phrase: this has been most interesting. He must end his work with a conviction (no matter how closely hedged about) on one side or the other, and this conviction must represent his most careful and impartial judgment. *Impartiality* not neutrality is the key to the correct, proper, and just presentation of history within the bounds of systematic study.

The student who has the courage to find and develop a historical problem, who has the mind and the patience to observe a critical method of research, who has the intellectual honesty to write without conscious bias and with conviction —this man will not only be adding to his capacities as a responsible citizen, he will be exercising his right of free inquiry. He will be enjoying a privilege for which America was founded and a right for which men are dying this very year. The succeeding chapters will develop these ideas more fully and will try to relate them specifically to the problems of the college student who has taken up his first serious piece of historical research and writing.

# CHAPTER II

# Finding the Perfect Topic

So far these pages have been devoted to discussing history as an abstraction, as a social service, and as a discipline. But the object of this book was otherwise. Primarily it was intended to help the beginner who did not know how to start his research, and to convince him that the writing of a serious essay is one of the most pleasant and rewarding things a person can do. Granted that finding a topic is oftentimes a discouraging business, and that the early stages of any research may be boring, just about everyone who gets immersed in a job of investigation agrees that it is fun. There are few thrills comparable to discovering errors in the authoritative works, to finding new source material in an odd place, and being able to give a new twist to an old hypothesis. There are few satisfactions equal to feeling oneself the master of an incident of the past, of being so well informed about it that, with a time machine, one could enter into the situation and play an intelligent part in it. There is no pleasure comparable to hitting upon a conclusion from a set of new data and then finding the inference indisputably established in a well-known but hitherto misunderstood document. Everyone who goes into a research project with the stamina to survive the first disappointments is almost bound to emerge with these warm and self-sufficing pleasures.

The first part of the beginner's work is the hardest and least rewarding. To find a proper subject may be sufficiently difficult to kill a good part of his enthusiasm and interest. There is no virtue in trying to conceal the difficulties. He will soon perceive them himself and will see that they are akin to those of the amateur geologist who is looking for a mine-site. Everywhere he looks, he sees possible ground, and his very freedom to look everywhere is one reason why he sees no point in digging at any given spot. But if he understands this, and realizes that his problem though difficult is not hopeless he will at least have made the first and most essential assault.

Suitable topics simply do not reveal themselves, and generally speaking, may not be revealed by another person. They are discovered by hard and oftentimes tedious work; seldom do they appear until the searcher has read extensively in areas of unimaginative historical writing, or until he has acquired that thing mysteriously called background, plainly called familiarity.

To come upon a proper topic, the student who has no natural predilections must first make a few broad decisions. He must decide what history interests him most. Is he most interested in any one of the national histories—American, English, French, German and so on; within the national category is he most interested in the medieval or modern periods; and within the time category does he prefer political, economic, social, or intellectual history? Once he has reached a decision within each of these brackets he may inquire further into his natural preferences.

But if the student has a hobby and if this hobby is sufficiently engrossing to lead him into one of its academic aspects, the problem is relatively easier. Does he collect stamps, or pictures of locomotives, or Staffordshire dogs? Does he like to read about hawking, exploration, or aviation? Has he a serious interest in Renaissance sculpture, Salvador Dali, Palestrina, Frank Lloyd Wright, or Nijinski? If he has a hobby some aspect of it can be easily made into a valid subject of historical research. There is no reason why a philatelist might not study any one of the thousand sides of the history of postal services; the locomotive bug, one of the sides of railroading; the amateur of painting, some phase of the history of art.

Whether he has a special field of interest or not, the chances are good that his first move should be in the direction of general reading. And unless he has a good general knowledge and is fairly familiar with the large aspects of his subject, he should begin with a textbook or similar book of reference. There are thousands of books of this kind and the student's adviser will know the right one.

At this suggestion many may balk. They will object to accepting a method of study which begins with the general and works towards the particular. They may even say that there is no sense in going to the particular after the mind's inventiveness has been dulled by too much contact with other people's ideas. They may assert that to send a student to a general work first is the sure guarantee that he will never see anything but the textbook writer's hypotheses, no matter if he pushes his research down to primary sources. In this argument there is wisdom, but its virtues appear to diminish in the light of realism and experience. For if any but the superior student were flung mercilessly into a large amount of primary data and told to find a topic there, he would have no idea of what he was looking for. Discouraged he would go back to the office of his adviser for further instructions, or with a plea to change his subject. Students who lack background must get it before they will have courage enough, energy enough, and the feeling of familiarity necessary to lead them into original work. So while there are dangers involved in working from the general to the specific, this method is the only one really defensible in terms of the ability of the average student. Therefore the student should bravely prepare himself for a little improving boredom and begin his general reading.

Depending upon his knowledge of the field the student should put in his first hours' efforts in going through the simplest and briefest accounts. Then he should read a longer and more detailed book in the same field, and perhaps a third and fourth. One theory of learning holds (and with good cause) that repetition is an essential part of the business. Whether this theory is scientifically provable or not, the average student would do well to subject his mind to the same material presented from several divergent points of view.

As he reads he will find himself becoming familiar with the political setting, the economic arrangement, the social milieu, and the intellectual values. Unconsciously he will start recognizing bits of the story and anticipating what is coming next. And this pleasure of recognition is no small thing. Actually it is powerful enough to drive travelers back to places they have seen again and again, and readers to books they have read a dozen times. To give oneself the gratification of being wise before the fact is the most pleasant and least vicious form of self-flattery. One will have the thrill of associating events with names, and names with characters; he will begin to associate laws with opinion, policies with economic and social compulsions. The age and the society will miraculously come to life, and some special phase of the living whole is bound to interest him more than others. This is the moment he has been waiting for; he should know now that he is about to find his topic.

Arrived at this happy place the student is ready for the next block of reading. This should be far more specialized; it should bear directly on the subject about which he wants to know more. He can go to any or all of the large co-operative survey works [1] and read the parts he sees to be relevant, or he can go to general works which deal with specific fractions of human history, such as studies in morals, economic history, social and intellectual movements. These are particularly recommended where the embryonic topic is not from straight political history. They will provide two important benefits: introduction to the details of the subject; introduction to the literature about it. Let us discuss the first of these.

Knowledge of the intricacies is an absolutely essential first step, for only with such knowledge can the student hope to begin limiting his topic. The subject which he chose to study because it seemed easy at first glance now becomes involved, and the more complicated it becomes, the greater the necessity to detach and concentrate on some manageable fragment. Only as he does this will his subject become fit for a serious essay.

1. The most important of these are:

   I. General

     1. J. B. Bury and others, eds., *The Cambridge Ancient History* (12 vols. Cambridge, Eng., and N.Y., 1923–39).

     2. Planned by J. B. Bury. H. M. Gwatkin and others, eds., *The Cambridge Medieval History* (6 vols., N.Y., 1924–36).

     3. Planned by Lord Acton. A. W. Ward and others, eds., *The Cambridge Modern History* (14 vols., Cambridge, Eng., and N.Y., 1902–12; reprinted without bibliography and atlas, 13 vols., Cambridge, Eng., and N.Y., 1934).

     4. Ernest Lavisse and Alfred Rambaud, eds., *Histoire générale du IVᵉ siècle à nos jours* (12 vols., Paris, 1893–1901).

     5. Hans Freyer and others, eds., *Propyläen-Weltgeschichte* (10 vols. and 1 index vol., Berlin, 1929–33).

     6. Louis Halphen and P. Sagnac, eds., *Peuples et civilisations* (18 vols. to be 20 vols., Paris, 1926–37).

   II. United States

     1. A. B. Hart, ed., *The American Nation: A History from Original Sources by Associated Scholars* (28 vols., N.Y. and London, 1904–18).

     2. Allen Johnson, ed., *Chronicles of America* (50 vols., New Haven, 1918–21).

Let us assume that from a reading of the textbooks and the larger survey works the student recognizes an old hobby or finds a new interest in railroads. When he first hits upon this as an interesting topic he boldly proposes to write an essay on the history of the *Baltimore and Ohio Railroad.* He has made his first decision on the matter, but certainly not his last. For his next reading is bound to reveal to him the enormous size of his topic, if not that an excellent two-volume work on it has already been written. Obviously it will be impossible to try to do a proper piece of work on so large a thing, and so, delaying judgment, he reads further in the history of the B & O. This is his second decision and his first tentative limitation of his broad topic.

---

    3. A. M. Schlesinger and D. R. Fox, eds., *History of American Life* (12 vols., N.Y., 1927– ).

    4. R. H. Gabriel, ed., *Pageant of America: A Pictorial History of the United States* (15 vols., New Haven, 1925–29).

III. General Europe

    1. W. L. Langer, ed., *The Rise of Modern Europe* (6 vols. published to date [1941] to be 20 vols., N.Y., 1934– ).

IV. England

    1. William Hunt and R. L. Poole, eds., *Political History of England* (12 vols., London and N.Y., 1905–10).

    2. Charles Oman, ed., *History of England* (8 vols., London and N.Y., 1904–34).

    3. G. N. Clark, ed., *The Oxford History of England* (7 vols. published to date [1941] to be 14 vols., Oxford, 1934– ).

V. France

    1. Frantz Funck-Brentano, ed., *Histoire de France racontée à tous* (11 vols., Paris, 1911–33). Translated into English.

    2. Gabriel Hanotaux, ed., *Histoire de la nation française* (15 vols., Paris, 1920–29).

    3. Ernest Lavisse, ed., *Histoire de France depuis les origines jusqu'à la révolution* (9 vols. in 18., Paris, 1900–11).

    4. Ernest Lavisse, ed., *Histoire de France contemporaine depuis la révolution jusqu'à la paix de 1919* (10 vols., Paris, 1920–22).

VI. Germany

    1. Hans von Zwiedineck-Südenhorst, ed., *Bibliothek deutscher Geschichte* (24 vols., Stuttgart and Berlin, 1876–1912).

More study of the subject may well reveal that building a railroad was complicated—the early railroaders had problems of surveying a route, of acquiring a right of way, of buying rails and ties, of labor, of government subsidy, and the like. Any one of these problems is good for an essay topic, and the student, let us assume, for personal reasons makes his third decision and elects to write on the labor problem. His focus is narrowing and his topic is becoming more and more manageable, but he has not yet completed the process of limitation.

Going deeper into the railroad's labor problem must show him that the problem was not the same in all years of the railroad's history, nor was it the simple thing he imagined it. More decisions to limit and more limitations must follow. And then somewhere along this line of action the student will hit upon the perfect topic. Sufficiently small it will be to fall within his intellectual grasp, sufficiently important when properly oriented to be history not antiquarianism, sufficiently close to his heart to interest him, and sufficiently easy to permit him to do a workmanlike job. But before going farther into the nature of this splendid thing, the second benefit of more detailed reading must be set forth.

Ostensibly the detailed and specific studies already referred to were written by scholars; they were therefore composed with becoming academic modesty. The men who wrote them in effect say to the reader, "This is the way it all appeared to me, but since you, reader, and I are both working in the same cause, I want to tell you how I arrived at these conclusions." The author does two things to convince the reader of the genuineness of his purpose: one, he tells in footnotes where his information came from; again, he appends at the end of his volume a bibliography of the general and special works, and the source materials which he thinks useful for further and more detailed study. This bibliography is of greatest benefit in proceeding to the last phase of research. It makes possible not merely the discovery but also the working out of the perfect topic.

Certainly the perfect topic needs definition. In the first place it should, where possible, be a fragment of the past which the student has himself found interesting. The man who was allergic to the old masters or constitutional law would be a fool to take a subject in these fields even if he saw he could swiftly finish it up and be done with it. His pains of study and construction would far outweigh his pleasure of getting the job done promptly, and if the task were sufficiently uncongenial he might never get it done even though it seemed easy at first glance. Historical research can be fun, and there is no virtue in making it torment. The student ought to think of his topic with a pride akin to paternity. When he feels like telling his friends about his research, when he goes around referring to so and so as my man, when he realizes he could spend two hours in a barroom of the day and not be known as Stranger, then he has his subject.

In the second place, however, this topic must suit the student's ability. It is possible that his amateur or dilettante interest will lead him into a field which proves far too difficult for him and in which he is completely lost. A man who went into the subject of French democracy in the 1830's because of a boyhood admiration for Louis Blanc might find that to define the very term democracy led him into sociology and political theory, of which he was totally ignorant. Rather than bash his head against these unknown disciplines, he would do much better to shift his interest to some more tangible phase of Blanc's long and eventful life.

In the third place certain negative things about the perfect topic should be said. Students are all too apt to consider such phenomena as political parties, wars, elections, and constitutions as the proper stuff of history; and pants buttons, incandescent lamps, gold fish, and circuses as not history at all.

People who hold this view are defining history with a lethal narrowness. They should be reinformed that anything which has impinged upon the life of man and left its impress there is a valid part of the study, and the perfect topic with certain reservations might just as well be "The Clothes of the Settlers of Massachusetts," or "Beginnings of the Manufacture of Mousetraps," as "The Presidential Election of 1936." But lest this statement be taken too literally one must pause for the reservations.

Topics may be equally good as exercises in research and differ widely in ultimate importance. If the writing of history has a social function, the chances are that the investigation of a presidential election will be of more social moment than one dealing with killing mice. Next, it should be observed that if any small and relatively unimportant phase of existence is studied without any reference to its place in the general social panorama, it will have nothing much more than an antiquarian value. That is, a man who wrote about mice and mousetraps as if mice were *not* a source of woe to mankind, and as if the making of mousetraps were *not* an important economic activity for a small group of people, and as if the execution of mice were *not* something more than a random pursuit of unidentifiable persons—this man would not be writing history at all. But a simple understanding of obligation, and a realization that the war between mice and men is an integral though small part of the large sphere of living, would permit a student to place his tiny study in correct historical perspective and make a valid contribution to our knowledge of the past.

A fourth quality of the perfect topic and one already fairly well defined is its restrictedness. Briefly let it be said that the student has not a whole lifetime at his disposal, and in order to do a systematic piece of work and derive therefrom the pleasures and benefits already set forth, he should be satisfied with a topic rigorously limited in time and space. If he insists on a large one like "Church and State in the Middle Ages," or "The History of Taxation," or "The Effect of Rainfall on the Development of China, Japan, and Korea," he cannot hope to do much more than plagiarize a textbook. This is not an improving activity. If on the other hand he limited himself to "Church, State, and the Coronation of Hugh Capet," or "The Tax on Doors and Windows in France," or "Rainfall and Kansas Corn," he might well have possession of the much-pursued thing.

The perfect topic has a fifth characteristic: its source material should be written in a language that the student can read. If the student does not know a word of French, he may have a hard time finding a reputable subject in French history. If he knows a little French and is willing to use it, he will certainly get a thrill out of putting his knowledge to practical use.

True, certain bits of history belong to the world, and large amounts of their source materials have been translated into English. If the student's adviser can indicate such an area in the history of some non-English-speaking race, a very good, but not perfect, topic may be found. It should be said that the ordinary modern language requirements of most colleges are a guarantee that the student can read historical prose of that tongue. Frequently he will be gratified to find how much easier it is to read straight historical narrative than the *belles lettres* of his language courses. He will find the vocabulary smaller and the sentence structure less complex.

A final quality of the perfect topic is its workability. By this is meant the physical ease with which it may be studied. There are an infinite number of perfect topics to the abstract man, but to the specific man living in New York, Chicago, Washington, or New Haven, there are a limited number. This specific man is going to be physically curtailed by the limitations of his library, and no matter how alluring a topic may be, it must first and foremost be capable of development from the sources available to him. If the library lacks the material necessary for the topic, obviously the average undergraduate will not have the time to travel to one where it is to be found. To this matter however there is an interesting corollary. Nearly every library has its special and unique collections, and many of these have never been used for research of any sort. Nothing pleases librarians and donors so much as to have these collections serve the properly qualified researcher. If the student's library boasts this sort of accumulation, let him by all means seek it out, use it, and in so doing legitimately exploit the bibliographical advantages of his university.

# CHAPTER III

# Elements of Research

No perfect topic can be developed into a research project unless the student is willing to find out all he can about the literature which relates to it, and right from the start of his reading he must make a collection of book titles. This is his bibliography. The success or failure of his essay will in most cases depend upon the vigor and intelligence with which he gathers up titles of the articles and books which bear upon his subject. He gets them wherever he can: from his reading of special studies and scholarly works, from printed bibliographies, from reading lists, from the library's card catalogue, from the suggestions of his adviser. If he is the pupil of one school of historical method he will try to gather what he considers a complete list of books before he reads any of them. He will try to do all his bibliographical work at the start, so that he will not have to worry about the ugly subject again. There is more than a little perversity about this procedure. For if it is followed the student will find himself possessed of a staggering list of reading, some of which is utterly worthless, some of which is repetitive, much of which he can never read. Again in listing a "complete" bibliography at the start, the student will tend to close his eyes to the titles of other books which he finds in the later stages of his research. These may well be the most essential ones.

23

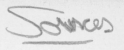

Getting a bibliography together, like research, is an organic process. It is one of those phenomena which is so closely bound up to others that it cannot be separated from them. The proper way to go about making a bibliography is to fuss over it as little as possible. The thing should grow with one's research, not precede it.

When the student begins reading his first detailed work he should keep his eye peeled for the footnote reference. Paragraphs he finds particularly germane to his topic will frequently be footnoted, and in the note there will usually appear the name of a book. This sort of book belongs in his preliminary bibliography. He should note its author and title, and when time permits, should glance through it; it may be of no use to him at all, or it may be the one important book for his purposes. If the latter, he should dive into it and note its bibliographical content. It is in this way that bibliographies fatten.

However this is by no means the only way it can grow. There are many other bibliographical aids which the careful student should make use of, and these should be called upon at the point where he is ready for them. They are such things as the famous printed guides to the multifarious historical literatures.  The single one of these which all students should know about is the well-known *Guide to Historical Literature* edited by G. M. Dutcher and others.[1] It not only lists all the important general and special studies in the field of historical literature, but also contains the titles of hundreds of lesser bibliographies.  If the student's topic is one which comes within the ambit of the *Encyclopedia of the Social Sciences*,[2] he can get admirable bibliographical help by looking up the notes which follow each article in the work. Of course he will

1. N.Y., 1931.
2. E. R. A. Seligman and Alvin Johnson, eds. (15 vols., N.Y., 1930–35; reprinted 1937, 15 vols. in 7).

have to use his head to get the most out of these volumes, but a little imagination will pay large dividends.

For general American history there is the well-known Channing, Hart, and Turner,[3] to be supplemented by Larned [4] and Griffin.[5] Solon J. Buck's résumé article is exceedingly useful.[6] In the field of American social history, the volumes of the Schlesinger and Fox [7] series contain excellent material. For the diplomatic and economic history of the United States, the student should go to the work of Bemis and Griffin,[8] and textbooks of Faulkner [9] or Shannon [10] or Kirkland.[11]

The best work on the sources of Medieval English history is Gross [12] though some twenty-five years have passed since the last revision. An up-to-the-minute edition is in progress. Paetow's volume [13] is certainly the best for the whole broad

3. Edward Channing and others, eds., *Guide to the Study and Reading of American History* (rev. ed., Boston and London, 1912). Not a critical bibliography.

4. J. N. Larned, ed., *Literature of American History* (Boston, 1902).

5. G. G. Griffin, *Writings on American History* (an annual bibliography begun in 1906, Washington, D.C., 1906-    ).

6. "The Status of Historical Bibliography in the United States," *The Pennsylvania Magazine of History and Biography*, vol. 63 (1939), 390-400.

7. A. M. Schlesinger and D. R. Fox, eds., *History of American Life* (12 vols., N.Y., 1927-36).

8. S. F. Bemis and G. G. Griffin, *Guide to the Diplomatic History of the United States 1775-1921* (Washington, 1935). The footnotes in S. F. Bemis, *A Diplomatic History of the United States* (N.Y., 1936) and the short notes at the chapter endings of T. A. Bailey, *A Diplomatic History of the American People* (N.Y., 1940) are full of valuable bibliographical data.

9. H. U. Faulkner, *American Economic History* (4th ed., N.Y. and London, 1938).

10. F. A. Shannon, *Economic History of the People of the United States* (N.Y., 1936).

11. E. C. Kirkland, *A History of American Economic Life* (rev. ed., N.Y., 1939).

12. Charles Gross, *Sources and Literature of English History from the Earliest Times to about 1485* (2nd rev. ed., London and N.Y., 1915).

13. L. J. Paetow, *Guide to the Study of Medieval History* (rev. ed., N.Y., 1931).

field of medieval studies. Three admirable and full books on the literature of the Tudor, Stuart, and early Hanoverian periods are those of Read,[14] Davies,[15] and Grose.[16] Grose's recent article in the *Journal of Modern History* supplements the work of his book.[17] D. J. Medley and Stanley Pargellis are preparing at the moment their *Bibliography of British History: 1714–89.* Excellent bibliographies of a general kind are included in the volumes of the new Oxford history.[18] The collaborative works, Shakespeare's England,[19] Johnson's England,[20] Early Victorian England,[21] and Whiteley's Wesley's England [22] contain splendid bibliographical material in the field of English social history, while the books of Cunningham,[23] Lipson,[24] Mantoux,[25] and Clapham [26] will adequately serve in the sphere of economic history.

The French have gone about the bibliography of their history in a complicated and disorderly fashion. Their great works on

14. Conyers Read, ed., *Bibliography of British History: Tudor Period, 1485–1603* (Oxford, 1933).

15. Godfrey Davies, ed., *Bibliography of British History: Stuart Period* (Oxford, 1928).

16. C. L. Grose, ed., *A Select Bibliography of British History, 1660–1760* (Chicago, 1939).

17. XII (1940), 515–534.

18. G. N. Clark, ed., *The Oxford History of England* (7 vols. pub. to date [1941] to be 14 vols., Oxford, 1934–   ).

19. No editor (2 vols., 1st ed. Oxford, 1916; several subsequent printings).

20. A. S. Turberville, ed. (2 vols., Oxford, 1933).

21. G. M. Young, ed. (2 vols., London, 1934).

22. J. H. Whiteley (London, 1938).

23. William Cunningham, *Growth of English Industry and Commerce* (2 vols. in 3, 5th and 6th rev. eds., Cambridge, Eng., 1922–29).

24. Ephraim Lipson, *Introduction to the Economic History of England* (London, 1915).

25. Paul Mantoux, *The Industrial Revolution in the Eighteenth Century* (rev. ed., N.Y., 1935).

26. J. H. Clapham, *An Economic History of Modern Britain* (3 vols., 2nd ed., Cambridge, Eng., 1930–38).

the subject are for the most part listed on pages 563 and 564 of the Dutcher and others, *Guide*,[27] and will not be reproduced here. The undergraduate need not consult these master works until his research is well advanced, and in the meantime he can find great bibliographical assistance in the books of the Lavisse series,[28] in Emile Bourgeois's Modern France,[29] in the economic studies of Sée,[30] Dunham,[31] and Clapham,[32] and in the bibliographical notes in the Langer series.[33] R. A. Winnacker has prepared and published in the *Journal of Modern History* the best bibliography of all phases of the French Third Republic.[34]

The bibliography of German history is contained in the famous Dahlmann-Waitz work,[35] which is probably too complicated to be of great use to the average undergraduate. Before he goes to this great compilation (it lists some 20,000 titles) he might do better to look through the proper bibliographical sections of the Cambridge Modern History.[36] The Dutcher and others *Guide* [37] is also extremely useful.

27. See note, page 24, for the full title of this book.

28. See note, page 17, V. France, 3, 4.

29. Emile Bourgeois, *History of Modern France: 1815–1913* (2 vols., Cambridge, Eng., 1922).

30. Henri Sée, *La Vie économique de la France sous la monarchie censitaire* (Paris, 1927). There is an English translation.

31. A. L. Dunham, *The Anglo-French Treaty of Commerce of 1860 and the Progress of the Industrial Revolution in France* (Ann Arbor, 1930).

32. J. H. Clapham, *The Economic Development of France and Germany, 1815–1914* (4th ed., Cambridge, Eng., 1936).

33. See note, page 17, III. General Europe, 1.

34. "The Third French Republic," *Journal of Modern History*, X (1938), 372–409.

35. F. C. Dahlmann and Georg Waitz, *Quellenkunde der deutschen Geschichte* (9th ed., E. Baasch and others, eds., Leipzig, 1931).

36. See note, page 16, I. General, 3. Note that the bibliographies are printed at the end of each volume and that they have been *omitted* in the latest popular edition (1934). There is a plan to bring them up-to-date and publish them as a separate volume in this edition.

37. See note 1, page 24.

The best introduction to the bibliography of European diplomatic history can be found in Bourgeois,[38] Immich,[39] Wahl,[40] Langer and Armstrong,[41] Langer,[42] and Seton-Watson.[43]

Besides consulting these monuments the student has other significant ways of adding to his knowledge of relevant literature. Intelligent use of a library's card catalogue is one that is particularly important. Stack privileges, which permit him to wander through his library's collections, may be the most profitable of all bibliographical aids. But it should be said at once that libraries are unwilling to give everyone these rights, and that the unqualified student who wins them will be able to waste more time than he thought possible. He should not venture into the stack until he knows what he is about, and until he knows the kind of book he wants to find.[44] Numerous

38. Emile Bourgeois, *Manuel historique de la politique étrangère* (4 vols., Paris, 1892–1926).

39. Max Immich, *Geschichte des europäischen Staatensystems von 1660 bis 1789* (Munich, 1905).

40. Adalbert Wahl, *Geschichte des europäischen Staatensystems . . .*, *1789–1815* (Munich, 1912).

41. W. L. Langer and H. F. Armstrong, eds., *Foreign Affairs Bibliography* (N.Y., 1933).

42. W. L. Langer, *European Alliances and Alignments, 1871–1890* (N.Y., 1931), and *The Diplomacy of Imperialism, 1890–1902* (2 vols., N.Y., 1935).

43. R. W. Seton-Watson, *Britain in Europe, 1789–1914* (Cambridge, Eng., 1937).

44. There are a few useful rules for an exploration of the stack. Before going to this wasteland the student should get the names of a dozen books related to his subject. Their points of departure should differ, if possible— that is, the title of one should suggest a straight political approach; the title of another a philosophical approach; of others, an approach suggesting the sociological, the economic, the literary, and governmental. The student should look up the call numbers of these works, and then go to them in the stacks. Librarians try to shelve books according to subject and do so with great aplomb where the subject is a clear-cut affair. But the contents of many books would permit these books to be shelved in any one of half a dozen places, as history, philosophy, sociology, economics, literature, or government, for example. The result is that all the books the student de-

historical journals make a point of keeping up-to-date on new historical writing, and on the publication of source material. The student's adviser should be able to tell him which of the many he might go to with most profit. Poole's *Index to Periodical Literature* [45] and the *Readers' Guide to Periodical Literature* [46] are of indispensable aid in looking up contemporary comment on historical events. These great indexes tell what magazine articles have appeared in American magazines since 1802. To be sure the first volumes of Poole are far less complete than the recent volumes of the *Readers' Guide* but are nevertheless an admirable help. Both of these reference works are most useful for research in subjects which have not yet become the province of the summarizing writer, and not yet been crystallized in book form. Especially topics of the moment may be investigated with the use of these tools.

The student should use all these aids and conveniences when his research demands, which takes us to the main problem of the chapter.

As has been said, historical research is much like research in the natural sciences. It consists of gathering facts—old and well-known ones at first, and later, with the help of deeper knowledge of bibliography, new ones. It consists of forming hypotheses on the basis of these facts, of testing these hypotheses for traces of one's own ignorance or bias, of cleansing them if possible. The goal of research is to build better hypotheses than al-

sires are scarcely, if ever, shelved as one compact group; rather they stand in many groups separated from one another by considerable distances. Only by realizing this, and overcoming it as suggested, can the student make good use of his stack privileges.

45. Published first in 1882, in 2 vols. which covered the period 1802–82 for about 250 magazines. Thereafter it appeared 1 vol. per year until 1906 at which time it ceased publication. Meanwhile *The Readers' Guide* had been going for 6 years.

46. The first volume of *The Readers' Guide* covers the period 1900–1904. It used only some 70 magazines, but at the present (1941) it uses some 110. It has been published steadily ever since.

ready exist and to establish them as relatively more true: it is to reveal a sharper picture of what happened and to make a closer approach to actuality than anyone has yet contrived. In the end, it results in giving to the world a new and original statement of what happened—original in that it is the student's very own contribution to human knowledge. Such a contribution was William Smart McKechnie's when he discovered that Magna Carta was not the foundation stone of English liberty as the men of the seventeenth century had claimed. What rights the great document did proclaim were rights to be enjoyed by the feudal group alone, and by no stretch of the imagination could they be extended to the vast bulk of the people who lived in nonfeudal status. Such a contribution was Frederick Jackson Turner's when he demonstrated that American democracy was largely a matter of life at the brink of a constantly moving *frontier* where there could be no privilege, and was not a simple matter of the innate American love of freedom.

Discussion of the best method of research is futile. Every student is bound to develop his own. About the only advice on the matter which can be tendered must come in the form of large general rules.

Assuming that the topic is a perfect one, and that the student has read enough in and around it to have arrived at a set of hypotheses, he should now set these down on a piece of paper. And here let us pause to exorcise once and for all any mystery attached to a "hypothesis." The word is admittedly formidable but the thing is one of the commonest in life. Every time the mind perceives a relationship between two things it creates a hypothesis. The sight of a running man creates the hypothesis "hurry"; the sound of a howling child creates the hypothesis "unhappiness." This habit of jumping at conclusions is one of the mind's most irrepressible activities, and without this perpetual and involuntary spark the mind would be no mind at all. A student who submits his intelligence to a set of data will find that whether he likes it or not the intelligence starts arranging the data into a pattern. This pattern may be then torn loose from the data, and stated as a conclusion. Sir James Barrie in *A Window in Thrums* gives as neat and pleasant an illustration of the force of hypothesis and of the fertility of mind of curious people who draw them as can be found in the official literature of philosophy and psychology.

For example a person who read the following facts: forty-six states for Roosevelt, two for Landon, would automatically conclude: victory for Roosevelt, even though no such flat statement appeared in the data. Now if he were writing about the United States in 1936, one of his hypotheses would be that Roosevelt was elected president. He would therefore be justified, for the time being, in setting this hypothesis down as a statement of fact. It would thereupon become one of the entries in his outline of the story of that year. And it would remain a statement of fact unless subsequent reading of more data showed him that his first conclusion were wrong. The main point to be understood is that there is nothing occult about hypotheses, and that one of the first and most necessary steps in research is to seize them as they appear and arrange them in a rough and simple order. They are now nothing more or less than the first outline.

In this guise they are far from sacrosanct; the student should be intensely suspicious of them and stand ready to change them as his knowledge increases. But their flimsiness does not mean that they are useless; quite the contrary, for in the main they will enable him to block out and advance upon his next batch of reading. That is, we are assuming that the topic, small as it is, permits itself to be broken down into subtopics and sub-subtopics. These are the fractions about which he wishes to learn, and he may do so by going ahead into selective or "relevant" reading.

By "relevant" reading is meant that reading directed specifically towards the proof or disproof of a hypothesis. The student may find this sort of material in a variety of ways. In the first place he makes a point of recording the titles of books cited in the footnotes of the special studies which he is already reading. He studies the bibliographical section of the work with his eye set for the proper title. Nor should he be too demanding about the title; there are books whose titles do not describe the content. Today I received a publisher's notice of a book called *And Still the Waters Run* [47] which he proclaims the "definitive . . . story of the dissolution of five Indian republics . . ." He should look at the book which now appears on the list. A few will be very close to his subject, and these he should skim through except for the pages which are of vital interest for him.

And here a parenthetic paragraph on skimming, which is a talent that every reader should cultivate. To be sure everyone skims telephone books, when looking up a number, and library catalogues, when chasing a book, but few people carry the art over into their reading habits. Skimming means reading to acquire a maximum of the book's content in a minimum of time. And scholars who are constantly in arrears in the literature of their subject are virtually forced to use it as one of their most essential techniques. Some develop into incredibly facile skimmers, and there are stories of the great Charles Homer Haskins ripping through four hundred pages of German in half an hour and of then being able to recount accurately the main arguments of the text. Theodore Roosevelt is said to have had the same gift.

Yet gift is scarcely the correct word, for probably these men and all others who can wolf the printed page got that way by deliberate intent and long practice. It is likely that one of them may have begun to gain speed in reading by the following method. He opened the book and looked at the title page; he noted the full title and the even more descriptive subtitle if there

47. Angie Debo (Princeton, 1940).

was one. *Germans in the Cameroons, 1884–1914*, title; *A Case Study in Modern Imperialism*, subtitle, he might find in Harry R. Rudin's book. Then he paused a moment to let the full meaning of the author's declaration of purpose soak in. Then he read the preface carefully. In this passage what further promises does the author make? Then he paused another moment while he tried to answer. Then he looked back at the table of contents. In what order will Rudin handle the problems he has spoken of? All right. And now he advanced into Chapter I, which is oftentimes nothing less than the extremely important introduction. These, the preliminaries, gave a good notion of what he was going to look for, and they gave him a passing familiarity with the key words, phrases, and expressions which the author was bound to use throughout. The rest was not so hard. With a certainty that he was missing the colorful detail and some of the fine distinctions, the reader began to leaf through with his eye set for the promised elaboration of the main ideas. And he found most of them because he already felt with some sureness that they would be associated with the key words and expressions. He paid great attention to the introductory and summary paragraphs of each chapter, to the first and last sentences of other paragraphs that looked good, and he read the conclusion at the end of the book with his mind at its sharpest. Then he asked himself, "Is there anything here that I want," and proceeded to take notes accordingly. After putting himself through this training, he got so that his skimming became both rapid and accurate, and he could go to a library stack and consume books by the yard. Of course he couldn't thus dispose of the ones which were directly on his subject, but at least he could and did spare himself the waste of reading thousands of pages of irrelevancy.

Whether the present student, the one who is reading this chapter, chooses to skim or not to skim, he ought to scour the book before him for more bibliographical suggestions. He will find that some of the titles he has collected begin to recur, and their very recurrence is strong evidence of their importance in the general field of his study. Next he will find that certain hypotheses begin to recur also. If he is keen he may be able to see that all authors are following a single one, and that the originator made a bad error of judgment. Perpetual suspicion and a flexibility of mind are virtues he should sedulously cultivate.

In the second place there are a number of tricks of the trade that will be of use to him at this stage in his work. For example, he should be on the alert for the names of prominent men and should take note of them. These names when properly used can be of great service in making his reading relevant. "Proper use" involves looking them up in various encyclopedias and biographical dictionaries.[48] The virtue in this lies in finding what official positions the man held, what his prejudices were, what books or memoirs, if any, he wrote. With these pieces of information the student may go to the man's own writings, may look up the proceedings of the societies he belonged to, may be able to find his speeches before legislative bodies or other organizations recorded in official government publications. If the man held a place in the foreign service his dispatches and reports might well be accessible in the many volumes of diplomatic correspondence which have been published.

48. a. *The Dictionary of American Biography* (20 vols. and index vol., N.Y., 1928–36). As the title suggests, deals with biography of Americans.

b. *The Encyclopedia of the Social Sciences* (15 vols., N.Y., 1930–35; reprinted 1937, 15 vols. in 7). Only useful with respect to men who have made considerable contributions to the world of history and social science.

c. *The Dictionary of National Biography* (63 vols. and 3 sup. eds. in 7 vols., London and N.Y., 1885–1927). Deals with the biography of Englishmen.

d. *The Encyclopedia Britannica* (29 vols., 11th ed. [the best] 1910–11). The inferior 14th ed. was published first in 1929 in 24 vols.

e. *Nouvelle Biographie générale* (46 vols. in 24, Paris, 1855–66). Chiefly useful for biographical information on men of early or mid-nine-

If the subject is bare of men's names, the student would do well to note the names of societies, clubs, and other organizations and pursue them through his bibliographical channels. He would be wise to note the exact dates of events, and, when possible, chase these to newspaper files, and magazine comment. Should his topic happen to touch upon legislative or judicial action, he should go to records of debate or trial. It is on wild-goose chases like these that the greatest discoveries often occur.

The following is not a great discovery, in fact not much of a wild-goose chase, but it does illustrate the point. A student, interested in the controlled elections of Louis Philippe's day, was reading the daily papers of the time. During the campaign of 1839 he noticed that the government was extremely generous to certain communities; that it allotted them sums of money to patch up the hospital, or build a quay, or mend a bridge. He noticed that sometimes these gifts came in the form of a portrait of the king to hang in the city hall, or a relic to put in the church. He noticed that one town received a handsome Gobelin tapestry. Gobelin was a state industry in the time of Louis XIV, he remembered; "I wonder if it still was in Louis Philippe's day?" He went to an encyclopedia and looked up Gobelin. Yes, it was still state-run, and there in the middle of the article was a

---

teenth century who were not of sufficient importance to make the later, more carefully edited biographical dictionaries.

f. *Grand Dictionnaire universel du XIXᵉ siècle* (18 vols., Paris, 1865–76; two sup. vols., 1878–84).

g. *La grande Encyclopédie* (31 vols., Paris, 1886–1902).

h. *Nouveau Larousse illustré* (7 vols. and 1 sup. vol., Paris 1898–1907).

i. *Larousse du XXᵉ siècle* (6 vols., Paris, 1928–33).

j. *Enciclopedia universal ilustrada* (70 vols. in 72 and 10 sup. vols., Barcelona, 1905–33). In Spanish and one of the best of all encyclopedias.

k. *Allgemeine deutsche Biographie* (55 vols. and 1 index vol., Leipzig, 1875–1912).

l. *Der grosse Brockhaus* (20 vols. and 1 sup. vol., Leipzig, 1928–35).

m. See also especially the various national editions of *Who's Who*, e.g., *Who's Who in America*, *Wer ist's*, *Qui êtes-vous*, etc.

list of the men who had been its directors. Naturally he read down to 1839, and there he found a vaguely familiar name. Was this man a deputy? The student found that he was. He also found that he was a staunch member of the "In" party. But most startlingly he found that the deputy was running for office from the very town which had received the tapestry. Here then was as good a circumstantial case of pork-barrel tactics as could be found. The director of the Gobelin studio was buying the allegiance of the voters of his district by presenting them with a tapestry which their own taxes had paid for. It was a small discovery, but it fitted into a general argument and lent it added strength.

In one sense much of the work done on both wild-goose chases and the more prosaic stretches of reading will not be strictly "relevant," yet in another undeniably it will be. For obviously all of this material cannot bear directly upon the narrow and restricted hypothesis which the student took as his point of departure. Just as plainly, however, only by following some such method, can the student hope to keep from dissipating his time and energy over a hopelessly broad field of investigation. This kind of reading then will be "relevant" in the best sense of the word. It will be sufficiently narrow to keep the student's nose to the topic, and sufficiently broad to cause him to weigh and ponder the validity of his first hypotheses from the vantage of a wide and variegated critical position.

There are certain mechanical sides to research that every student should know before he does even his first reading. And the most important of these is the business of taking notes. No one who hopes to write a critical essay can do so without making short abstracts of the information furnished him by his sources. And so notes must be kept. Habitually students begin by taking notes in a notebook. The notebook is the worst of all possible systems. For when filled with notes it will be most useful for writing if the notes have been taken in the order in which they are going to be used. Obviously when one starts his research, he has no exact conception of the structure of his forthcoming essay, and consequently is unable to read and take notes in any prearranged pattern. The ultimate effect of using a notebook then is to jumble on the same page information which bears on a half dozen hypotheses. And when the student comes to use these notes, he can do so only by turning the pages of his book back and forth with a fair chance of losing some of his most valuable material.

The best sort of note system is one which employs cards or small slips of paper cut in any one of the three standard sizes— three by five, four by six, or five by eight.[49] Stationers or paper houses will furnish these at very small cost, and will be able also to provide small and inexpensive filing boxes, and alphabetized or blank index cards. If one uses the card system, he should, to be consistent, endeavor to put no more than one fact on a card. This practice will permit him the greatest latitude in arranging his notes just before writing. It will also practically assure him a bed in a psychopathic ward. Very few people, and they, generally speaking, a race of note-takers, have the patience to be so painstakingly consistent. Probably the best advice to the beginner would be to take notes from a single reference on each card. If these notes contain a dozen facts, which bear upon a number of hypotheses, the student ought to enter this information at the top of the card. But remember, no matter how carefully the notes be taken, they are often completely inadequate, and the student may well have to go back to his source of information a half dozen times before he gets out of it all the things later investigation shows to be important.

Each card or slip, to be of real use, *must* always carry a

49. See Beatrice Webb, *My Apprenticeship* (London, 1926), Appendix C, pp. 426–436. E. W. Dow, *Principles of a Note-System for Historical Studies* (N.Y. and London, 1924). Be sure to see C. G. Crump, *History and Historical Research* (London, 1928), Chap. IV.

reference. That is, somewhere on the card, there must be a note, or symbol, or hieroglyph which stands for the name of an author, the title of his work, and the volume and page which has furnished the information inscribed on the card. But to this general practice there are permissible exceptions. Certain facts are so generally known—things like the dates of the battle of Hastings, and the end of the Holy Roman Empire—that to take references on them is ridiculous. Generally speaking, most of the material in the average textbook is not worth identifying as to author, title, and page, because the same material could be found in substantially the same form in a half hundred other books. However should the student wish to quote a textbook, or attack a textbook hypothesis, or use a table of statistics not found elsewhere, he should remember to write down the necessary data.

This will seem an exceedingly tedious duty at first, but will soon become second nature. It *must* be done. If the student refuses to keep such references, he will find himself in a mess of grave difficulties. For example, if he finds a situation interpreted in two different ways in two different books, he will be unable to tell which of the two he is to accept unless he can go back to the books and investigate their relative merits. If he has no references he will have little of the critical approach, he will be unable to footnote his own essay, and he will be unable to summarize his knowledge of the literature in his own bibliographical note.[50] If all these things are lost, he might better stop trying to write an essay.

Less important in the scholarly sense, though no less so in the utilitarian, is another admonition on note taking. Insofar as it is possible each slip should have in addition to the reference a

---

50. In this sense "bibliographical note" is a short essay in itself which comes at the end of the essay proper. It describes the literature which the student has used in his own research (see pp. 99–101 of this book where it is discussed at some length).

second bit of information. Ideally this should be a few words which indicate what phase of the large topic the note pertains to, where the note will be used in the essay, or upon what hypothesis it bears. These words are very hard to find, as hypotheses change the words become useless; they are boring to write; but even with all these obvious disadvantages they are worth trying. If the gods are smiling and the words are well chosen, the whole note system may be put in order in a very short time and the business of composing or blocking out undertaken with a heart-warming ease.

This last point should be qualified, and qualified notably with respect to the mental makeup of the student. If a student is new to research and the techniques of the scholar, he may find that it is virtually impossible to cut himself loose from his notes. Only when they are spread out before him can he write with speed and certainty. He is the man who can for a time, at least, afford to make a fetish of his note system, who can afford to cross-index it elaborately, to put things into it which he hopes later to incorporate piecemeal into his text. But the student who knows what he's about and has some of the balance and maturity of the finished scholar need not, in fact *must* not, stick too closely to his notes when he is writing. Writing history is an act of individual creation; it is not the simple patching together of bits of information gotten from the sources. The sardonic mot ascribed to Carl Becker: "If you take something from one book, it's plagiarism; if you take it from half a dozen, it's scholarship," is not strictly true. There must be *something added* to the material of one's research, a synthetic something that is wholly one's own. It is not to be won by continuous, intense, and myopic scrutiny of notes. It comes most often when the student is mentally exhausted from his study and has gone far away from his notes; it comes in the moments of rest and mental relaxation when he's listening to well-known music, or while he's shaving or taking a walk. It cannot be summoned voluntarily, for it is something that lies deep in the subconscious, far out of earshot of the voice of command. He can get it and make a masterpiece of his essay if he alternately ponders, forgets, ponders, and forgets.

So far this discussion of notes has been restricted to those which deal with the fact of the topic. There is however another kind—the bibliographical note—which demands some explanation. Each bibliographical note should be taken on a separate card. It should contain the author's full name (not just his last name), the full title of the book as it appears on the title page (not as it appears on the binding), the number of volumes, and the place and date of publication. This information might be called the skeleton of the note and in many cases where the qualities of the book are well-known it will suffice. But since bibliographical notes will be used when the student is writing up his bibliography, they should, in the main, also contain a sentence or two descriptive of the content of the book and of the author's point of view. The fact that an author is violently imperialist or anti-imperialist, Catholic or anti-Catholic, monarchist or communist is frequently as important to know as the title of his book, and any bibliography which does not mention the general scope of the various works, what they cover, what they omit, the particular biases, strong points, and weak points of the authors, is virtually worthless.

Sometimes the student will have occasion to look up the reviews of a work as they appeared in the scholarly journals or the *Book Review Digest*.[51] These reviews will oftentimes be useful in the determining of the author's bias, and accurate reference to the review may well be set down as a part of the bibliographical note.

51. First published for the year 1905 and since then has appeared at the rate of one vol. per year. It is more useful in telling where and when books were reviewed in the scholarly journals than it is successful in abstracting the reviews themselves.

In describing the methods and mechanics of research it might appear that I am urging students to finish it up before they begin writing. Nothing of the sort. Rather, I would insist that research and writing are inextricably tied to each other. The best historical work will be done when the student pauses in his research long enough to write down the fresh and new ideas that jump to his mind, to think out and write the artful transition he sees between two sections of the emerging essay, to summarize difficult and closely reasoned passages which at the moment he sees with clarity. Again the best writing comes when he stops long enough in the final draft to re-examine his material in the light of a new slant, to do additional research for the purpose of bolstering a sickly hypothesis, or giving specific identity to a mildewed generalization. The construction of the essay should progress along these lines; the essay like the bibliography should be a living organic thing right from the moment the first book is opened. The fun will come in watching it come to life and grow with the student's growing command of the subject, and with his continual reshaping of hypotheses from the vantage point of increased knowledge.

# CHAPTER IV

# Organizing Material

Writing is a form of expression. So homespun a truth is this assertion that it hardly seems worth making, yet long and painful experience with student essays and examinations would indicate that it is one of those peculiarly elusive truths which have been obscured by their very obviousness. But obvious or not, the student must grasp the idea in its full force before he will be able to do a commendable piece of writing.

For one thing he must realize that a thought expressed must be expressed in an understandable idiom. To all practical ends anything not understood might well be considered unsaid. And there is no excuse in holding that a thing is so complex that it cannot be clearly expounded. No matter how complex, if it is fully understood—and this is the very bull's-eye of the matter—any concept whatever may be stated without any shadow of obscurity. Obscurities are a product of shabby thinking and imperfect knowledge. A story about Dr. Osler, and probably apocryphal, has him say that when he could write a children's book on his current piece of abstruse research then and only then did he feel he had mastered the subject. There is always, however, the danger, to use Thomas Copeland's aphorism, that simplifying a complicated idea too much may change it into a simple one: simple, as in Simple Simon. But it is by no means an inevitable result.

If a person has been forced by the demands of his job or by an inner compulsion to write and write, he often arrives at the place where the expression of his ideas becomes an act of unconscious creation. Before he starts, he knows most of his problems and has solved them. He not only towers over his topic, but also he towers over his method. He sees the whole complex of the thought and the expression of it; he is able to rip off the first paragraph with a sure knowledge of the structure and content of all the rest. Changes which he makes later in his manuscript are merely grammatical or stylistic; seldom does he alter the basic pattern. This kind of person is rare and his talent extraordinary. Nearly always however, the talent is not so much a natural gift as an acquired capacity, and like other such capacities, it has been acquired through a basic knowledge of the formal rules. The chances are good that his first serious composition was a stiff and lifeless affair, and that he did not achieve any measure of grace, facility, or power until he had done an enormous amount of writing according to the laws. The injunctions therefore which follow are not the simple key to the best writing; they are merely the rules which most people have learned and observed, and which a few great writers have been able to break or forget.

Historical writing is usually the simple exposition of concrete matters. To be true exposition it must have as its prime characteristic *a continuous flow of clearly stated ideas.* In this respect it differs most essentially from, say, the writing of *belles lettres* and offers an even more useful practice ground for learning the principles of composition. For writing history breaks down the complicated business, and allows the writer to worry first about content, and then about the nuances of expression. Inasmuch as the number and variety of points to be taken up are limited by the unalterable facts of his research, the student's problems of presentation are comfortably framed within fixed boundaries. Unlike the novelist his first concern is not whether he is conveying the intended mood, or imagery, or pace by the proper use of words, rhythm, and the neat devices of rhetoric. His first concern is to express his ideas in such a manner as will be absolutely clear and compelling. If he gains this end, he will discover that his writing has also taken on a rugged and honest grace that he could not have achieved any other way. Look at General Grant's memoirs to find a perfect illustration.

On the other hand, the novelist and his technique command advantages which the historian may envy. For the novelist working in an uncharted area is completely free to say what he pleases and in some respects is freer than the historian to get at truth. The historian who has a hunch that a prominent states-man having had a humble beginning, owed his first successes in politics to being pushed forward by a woman of social pre-eminence, probably could not prove the point from the documents and would have to leave it unsaid. A novelist, and Trol-lope is the one in mind, could (and did) take this statesman, give him a new name, fictionize him, and then tell the detailed story of his rise to power. Wherever the documents were lacking, Trollope called upon his knowledge of the world and in the end he wrote a clearer and truer biography than the historian. But were the two biographees the same man?

To return to the writing of history, and the mastery of its two essences. How achieve continuity and clarity? The first and most important rule is to be sure you know what you want to say and the order in which you wish to say it. Writing out in full, patching and cutting, without any preliminary plan is an unnecessarily wasteful procedure. The writer can escape a tremendous amount of painful revision by doing several ab-breviated drafts of the essay while his large interpretive con-ceptions are jelling. These are outlines. As has been said earlier, they are made up of statements which are no more than the main and qualifying hypotheses of the essay. When the writer starts his work he has no hypotheses; as it progresses he begins to acquire them; and when he finally decides that he is ready to write, he has a great many. If he has been wise in the period of his research, he will have noted them down as he went along, he would have changed them from time to time, adding new ones, reorienting some of his old ones. If he has done this, he will certainly realize the evolutionary nature of his work and the evolutionary character of his outline. An outline must evolve.

For purposes of illustration let us assume that the student chooses as his subject *The Election of 1837 in France.* Let us assume that he decides to concentrate on this election as the most representative, the best documented, and the most vital of a dozen or so that he had cursorily looked into. Let us assume that his topic is the workable, interesting thing which has all the other touted advantages of perfectness.

Let us assume too that he begins his work with perhaps only three hypotheses. They are: There was an election in France in 1837; The "In" party won it; The "Out" party made considerable resistance. The first of these is basic; it will be the entry which is glorified by standing first and which later will become the essay's title. At this moment the essay is in its simplest state, and an outline of it would look like this:

The Election of 1837
    A. The hard-fought campaign of the "Outs."
    B. The victory of the "Ins."

The student might be wise to write the outline down in this form. At once he will see that his two entries are complex ones and may be broken down further. The new outline would then look like this.

    A. The campaign of the "Outs."
        1. hard-fought.
        2. party defeated.
    B. The campaign of the "Ins."
        1. (probably) hard-fought.
        2. victorious.

At about this point the student should go to his note box and its blank guide cards. On the tabs of these cards he ought to write his hypotheses. That is, one prominent card will be labeled "Out Campaign," another such card "In Campaign." On less prominently tabbed cards he may write his other main entries, and then file these in the order that they appear in the outline. Now when he begins his note taking he will know where his notes belong in the primary scheme and may file them away until he wants to elaborate his hypotheses. When he faces this necessity it is comparatively easy to add new guide cards and rearrange the old notes to fit the new order. Constant reshuffling of the notes will inevitably accompany the research he should now embark upon.

Let us assume that the primary materials at his disposal are newspapers, pamphlets, memoirs, and the proper governmental archives. With his eye set for the word "elections" he begins reading the newspapers day-by-day in the period of the campaign, and starts to find out how hard-fought the battle really was. He will begin taking notes on the subjects that bear upon his general topic. For the first hours of his work, each one of these notes will apparently have no relation to any of the others. One will tell of electoral activity in a southern city, another will mention the disenfranchisement of an improperly qualified voter, another will involve the candidature of a well-known figure, and so on. All of these notes may be dropped in his note box behind a guide card which bears the device "Out Campaign." His reading and noting will continue, when suddenly a new hypothesis appears. More often than not it will appear when he least expects it or when he least wants it. It will come when he is far from his desk full of notes, maybe when he is in a shower or at a concert. Who was running the "Out Campaign?" Wasn't there a directing force? What do all these references to a central committee mean? A little backtracking

through the newspaper file reveals an article which he missed—
a statement that an old parliamentary leader was acting as
president of a central electoral committee of the opposition.

At once he has a new hypothesis. It is the assumption that
there was a central organizing force. He may now make a new
entry in his outline, and put a new guide card in his filing box.
Hereafter he will have his eye set for other mentions of this
committee, and as he finds them he will write "Central Committee" or some such phrase at the head of each card he uses for
these references. Suppose now that his newspaper carries an
article in which the names of the committeemen appear: this
is a lead of great importance, for now he can use the technique
suggested earlier. He may see if any of these men left memoirs,
if any of them were members of the chamber of deputies, if any
of them spoke for the record. By using hints of this kind he may
come upon the very material he most needs for the story of the
development of this central committee.

An imaginative student would not be content with knowing
about the central organization. If such an institution existed, he
would argue, it would be effective only if it had the support and
sympathy of local committees. So without so much as a single
direct reference to a local organization, he could assume one
from common sense. Here is a new hypothesis. If wise he will
put it in the outline, fix the eye for reference to it, and continue
to leaf the newspaper. The outline and the guide would now be
like this:

A. The Campaign of the "Outs."
   1. hard-fought?
   2. the electoral machine
      (a) the central committee, personnel.
      (b) local organizations.
   3. defeat.
B. The Campaign of the "Ins."
   etc.

To elaborate this much further will be uselessly tedious, but let us hazard one more advance into this matter of research and the outline. Again without the aid of documents (horse sense is all that is necessary) the student may well increase the number of his hypotheses and broaden the front of his attack. A central committee of any sort is always created for the performance of certain definite functions. This committee is an electoral committee. Its prime duty is to win the election. How does it proceed to this end? Still not knowing for certain, the student will do well to assume that the committee must be largely concerned in directing the vote towards candidates who were sympathetic to the "Out" platform. He would be safe in this assumption because if he found that the central committee was *not* interested in this matter it was indeed a strange committee. To establish the committee's diffidence in this matter would be as important and as interesting as the more prosaic opposite. This is something which the good scholar does and the amateur must understand. Translated into advice it is this: from time to time, release your mind from the restrictions of the material and give it a chance to operate in the realm of unvalidated theory. Draw upon personal experience which has no bearing or only remote bearing upon the problem at hand; draw upon common sense and let it supply a number of tentative hypotheses.

Realize, for example, that events proceed as often out of simple human quirks as out of complex and devious reasons of state, and that an accepted and sacrosanct explanation may be overlabored as often as understated. By way of illustration consider the stiffening of the French foreign office in its relations with Germany in 1932. On exceedingly good authority it appears that Gustav Stresemann's memoirs which came out in that year were in no small measure responsible. For Stresemann, because of his liberal and conciliating attitude, had enjoyed the confidence of France as few of his German contemporaries, and as a result had been able to forward the Locarno treaties. By virtue of these Germany shook herself free of some of the shackles of Versailles and re-established herself as the moral equal, at least, of the other European powers. This was no small victory. It was won at the expense of a certain amount of French pride and was a testament of Aristide Briand's willingness to meet a conciliator halfway. Seven years later (three years after Stresemann's death) his memoirs were published, and in them he went out of his way to show how he had been able to bluff and fool Briand. He did not pose himself as an open-minded conciliator, but as a smart diplomat, smarter by far than his French and English opponents. The men in the French foreign office did not find this interpretation a flattering one and partially as a result, when occasion arose, began to be as severe with the Germans as they could.

Realize too that human institutions are generally older than suspected, and that hypotheses to this effect may pay out handsomely. It is sometimes said that Charles Gross made a reputation by pushing the coroner back two reigns in English history.

Once you have grasped a hypothesis, no matter where you got it, put it into the outline and mark it as tentative. If it is a reasonable one, and if a new assault upon the material leaves it unproved or disproved, this alone is an important result of research.

If the student is able to follow all these suggestions, in time he will have a box full of five by eight slips arranged behind guide cards and a handsome outline. Furthermore, he will have (if he followed the advice at the end of the last chapter) a substantial number of written pages, summaries, transitions, ideas, and the like which he can fit into the manuscript as he begins to write it.

If the number of notes is enormous, so large in fact that he cannot begin to remember them all even when they have been neatly done up in categories, he would be prudent to do one

*Draft*

last piece of organizing before he begins his draft. This involves the making of a last and carefully annotated outline. To do it he should first give every one of his notes a number. Next, he should start a new outline on a deeply-margined sheet of paper. As he unravels this outline hypothesis by hypothesis he should go to his notes and write their numbers opposite the relevant hypotheses. In this he will have insurance against leaving out important material. Also he may see that certain of his notes are capable of supporting two or three hypotheses, in which case he can put them to that use by no more complicated maneuver than jotting their numbers in the two or three indicated places. But whatever he does with his notes and outline, let him remember that sometime during this period of his work he must tear himself loose from their pressing immediacy, that he must leave his mind alone to mull over the data in quiet, and to produce its own inevitable miracle—the new synthesis.

So much for the *contents* of the outline and hence of the essay which are dictated ultimately by the facts which the student found in his research. But the *form* of the essay is marked by a very different set of circumstances. The word *form* here means the order and the distribution of emphasis and the coherence of the argument. Obviously the facts do not govern these things. The force which governs them is that very delicate intangible and individual thing, which we will call the author's sense of artistry.

# CHAPTER V

# Writing[1]

Earlier it has been said that writing is expression, and that successful expression is dependent upon the continuity and clarity of the thought. We might now say that these desirable characteristics may, even while the essay is still in outline form, be introduced into it by submitting the outline to a new kind of criticism—criticism from the point of view of order. What things should come first? Of the many entries in the outline, which will make the most interesting beginning and at the same time lead most naturally to the rest of the essay? To go back to the familiar example: Is it proper to begin the essay with a consideration of the "Outs"? Will a discussion of that party make the best introductory material and will it make consideration of the "Ins" more easy and natural? If so, by all means

1. There is a multitude of textbooks on writing; they deal with every side of the matter: the technique of composition, the laws of grammar and rhetoric, how the great writers have written, how you yourself should go about learning to write. Granted that you can't learn writing out of a textbook any easier than sculpture by correspondence, you may be able to draw useful hints from some of the following: Among the classics, Herbert Spencer's *The Philosophy of Style* (Boston, 1892; many other eds.) is one of the most helpful. Of recent publication: Joseph M. Thomas and others, eds., *Composition for College Students* (N.Y., 1937) is one of the most helpful all-around books in the field. Paul N. Landis, *Freshman Composition* (Boston, 1940) is at its best in the matters of grammar and punctuation. Other general handbooks are: Majl Ewing and others, *A Guide to Better*

begin with the "Outs." On the other hand, the "Ins" are of a good deal more constitutional importance; if there were no "Ins" there would be no government, therefore no election, and certainly no essay. To discuss the "Outs" before the "Ins" is to set the whole story on a somewhat artificial base. Is this justifiable according to the fact of history? Probably not. Is it justifiable for esthetic reasons? Probably yes, because putting the "Outs" first makes it possible to leave the more important "Ins" for the last and most important place. Yet again if the transition from "Outs" to "Ins" is going to be forced and awkward (but easy and smooth if the order was reversed), then there is good reason to reconsider the whole problem.

Suppose now that the eventual solution put the "Ins" first. Two things are very apparent about the party: in the first place it is an institution, and in the second, it is the subject of a narrative. What should come first, the analysis of the institution or the story of the campaign? Quite obviously the analysis. But how long should this be. If it is too short, it is worthless; if too long, it has usurped an improper amount of emphasis and the important matter of the campaign will dangle from it like the dewlap from a steer. Can the analytical section be broken down? Can a satisfactory amount of it be used at the start, and the remainder slipped bit by bit into the narrative section?

---

*Writing* (N.Y., 1940); Albert H. Marckwardt, *Scribner Handbook of English* (N.Y., 1940); Donald Davidson, *American Composition and Rhetoric* (N.Y., 1939). Easley S. Jones, *Practice Handbook in English* (N.Y., 1935) provides a series of short exercises which the student might find diverting and profitable to do.

Porter G. Perrin, *An Index to English* (Chicago, 1939) is a sort of dictionary or short encyclopedia for writers. Arranged alphabetically under key words, the book lays down the rules of grammar, rhetoric, and composition, and illustrates them from successful authors' works.

Paul Haines, *Problems in Prose* (N.Y., 1939) provides passages from the work of good writers, many of them historians, and shows the reader how to appreciate and emulate them. Theodore Morrison and others, eds., *Five Kinds of Writing* (Boston, 1939) is a group of selections without comment. Part III is made up of bits from the best work of historians.

Does this method of proceeding destroy the sweep of the narrative, does it improperly weaken the analysis?

This is the sort of question which should be asked, thought about, and answered before writing. The careful person who makes a long final outline will have a chance to solve not only the large problems of order and emphasis (those which involve the arrangement of whole sections or chapters) but also many of the smaller ones which occur within short sequences of paragraphs.

There is no rule book where these questions and answers are set forth; they may come from only one place: the author's sense of proportion, his feeling for presentation. How may he cultivate this sense?

First, he must realize that there is such a thing as a sense of order and that every satisfactory book he has read and every satisfactory lecture he has heard has been satisfactory because its creator possessed this sense. Next, the beginner must realize that he can cultivate it, and can, indeed, make it his own. He can do this by observing it in others. Let him dedicate some of his reading time to an observation of how paragraphs, chapters, and whole books are put together. Let him ask himself why the facts of a given piece of writing are arranged as they are. Let him go to a lecture of his favorite lecturer with ear set not for the content, but for the form. Let him try to analyze why the lecture had clarity and drama and why the lecture of another person was not as good. These are exercises of the mind which may well develop his sense of form and lead gradually to his possessing it. Once this feeling of order is his, the main structural problems of composition should not be hard to solve, and a clear workmanlike essay ought almost to piece itself together. But no matter how good the composing may be, its forcefulness, even its very meaning, will be hopelessly dulled unless the writing itself is in accord with a few direct rules. If the composing art may be called the architecture of the essay, these next rules are no more than the "do's" and "don'ts" of, say, the carpentry or plumbing.

The writing of the essay is putting drapery on the skeletal outline. That the prose should be esthetically satisfactory to the reader is very important. Unfortunately you cannot tell people how to write any more than you can tell them how to paint a landscape or model a figure.[2] Beyond the obvious: "Realize the difficulty of writing with clarity; strive for clarity; and practice writing as you would music or tennis or drawing," you can only offer negative instruction. Observe the following "don'ts."

Don't use stilted language. When you want to say that Woodrow Wilson became angry do not say he *waxed wrathy*. Using words like this and other semiarchaic words and expressions like *meet* for *fitting*, *must needs do something* for *felt compelled to do something*, is not the proper way to please a modern reader. Do not use phrases which you know to be dignified and sober; nine times out of ten they are clichés of the worst sort, and clichés, like some slang, are the certain evidence of sloppy thinking.

Look out for these clichés. Do not say such things as "brought to a head," "bore fruit," "sheds light upon," "cut of his jib," "woods for the trees." For anyone who has followed Frank Sullivan and the cliché expert in the *New Yorker*, or who knows Gelett Burgess's, *Are You a Bromide?* this type of rubberstamp expression has taken on explicit terrors. However there are times when the way around a cliché is so forced that the remedy is worse than the disease. But in the main if you cannot think of a good way around you might do well to beat your pen into a plowshare and take up farming.

2. Three very good discussions of the art of writing are: Arthur Quiller-Couch, *On the Art of Writing* (N.Y., 1916); Percy Marks, *The Craft of Writing* (N.Y., 1932); and C. E. Montague, *A Writer's Notes on his Trade* (London and N.Y., 1930).

Avoid what H. W. Fowler calls the *elegant variation*.[3] If you are describing some thing or some person and you have to use the word or the man's name over and over again, do not feel impelled to use a different synonym at each mention. The obvious best substitute—where one is necessary—is the pronoun.

Avoid those words in current collegiate slang which have little or no precise meaning. For example the word "meat ball" is used now as a term of disapproval when applied to a fellow man. But exactly what the qualities of a "meat ball" are is very difficult to discover. Some people say he is dishonest, some say he is honest but stupid, some say he is a grind who doesn't get his hair cut often enough, some say he is disagreeable. After hearing the word applied indiscriminately to fifty kinds of person, you conclude that it only serves to describe those traits of human character which the user dislikes. In such circumstances it has almost as many meanings as users, and therefore no real meaning at all. There are unfortunately a great many terms of this kind, and their constant and irresponsible use goes far towards reducing speech to a mad jingle of sound.

But remember that not all slang is vapid. The American language is an unusually elastic one and is always in the process of adopting new words and expressions. Do not hesitate to use them when the situation is made to order, but see to it that you do not pull them in by the heels, nor use them because you are too lazy to discover a more precise term. By all means read H. L. Mencken's *The American Language* and pattern your own not on his vocabularies but on his philosophy of speech. It is conceivable that words from the sport pages, from trade journals, and *Variety* may be used with greatest effect if they are used naturally and unostentatiously.

3. H. W. Fowler, *A Dictionary of Modern English Usage* (London, 1934). This is a book which every writer should read through, or, if he is not sufficiently robust to carry out the assignment, a book which he should have as close to him as his dictionary.

Beware of the metaphor. Granted that it is always tempting to describe one thing in terms of another, try not to do it. Every once in a while the opportunity for the proper use of simile and metaphor appears, but even here try to hold back. If you cannot, at least see to it that the thing is done quickly. Compare England to the whale and Germany to the elephant if you must, but stop there. Do not go on to describe England's industry as a cetacean digestive process, and Germany's electoral system as elephantine. Far better than using a sad old cliché like the elephant-whale, draw your metaphors and similes from your own intimate experience. Compare Napoleon's Austerlitz to a fugue by Bach if you are musical, or say he raged through central Europe like a mad, untracked 2–8–8–4 Mallet if you love locomotives; but whatever you do, don't say he burst upon Europe like a wolf on the fold. You never saw a wolf outside a zoo; certainly you never saw one assault a fold—whatever that is. Perhaps the most tedious thing you can do is to overwork a figure of speech. Not only is it tedious, but often destructive of your narrative, for your reader may be so taken up with the figure that he neglects to follow the argument you hoped to make clear. Then again there is always the danger of scrambling the figure and coming out with something ridiculous: "The milk maid putting butter in a churn like the bee packing honey in the comb with its head."

Begin writing your paper with a vow to use the passive voice as seldom as possible. Well indeed has it earned its name. Its use makes a straightforward narrative unnecessarily difficult, and if employed over a long stretch of writing, it has the effect of muting the sharpness of the prose. It is an attractive device because it allows the writer to escape full responsibility for blunt statements. Granted that he may be reluctant to assume this responsibility, nevertheless passing it on to a nonexistent "it," is not the proper way out. Sometimes the passive is unavoidable: use it, but be sure first that no other device will do.

It is sad to offer nothing more substantial as stylistic guides than these few "don'ts." However they are about the only ones which may be offered generally. Everyone must individually develop his own "do's," and they must remain incontestably his own individual property. Wallace Notestein says that he tries to write as he speaks—only more tersely and more exactly. This is his method of composing. It may well be worth passing on; some reader of these pages may find it exactly suited to his temperament and ability, and may profit greatly by it. But what is good for one will not be good for all, and if you find this particular "do" unsatisfactory, try to write like John Milton, or E. B. White, or H. L. Mencken.

Beyond style there are phases of essay writing which are subject to instruction. They are the phases which have to do with the workmanship of construction, and in a certain unsubtle way they lend themselves to technical explanation. If continuity and clarity are really important to the expressiveness of the essay (and they most certainly are), there are mechanical ways of achieving them.

In the first place there is the matter of introduction. Its essential purpose is to draw the reader gradually and smoothly from his own separate existence into the realm of the essay; to lead him, for example, quietly and gently from his Franceless and electionless world into one made up exclusively of France and elections. The introduction's ultimate function is thus to guarantee the reader a continuity of intellectual experience. To achieve this is not hard. The first thing required is that the student realize that he has the reader at a great disadvantage.

If the writer has done a month's hard research the chances are good that he knows the subject more intimately than most of his readers. He knows the background; he knows the personalities; he knows the literature. He forgets that his own knowledge of the subject has grown enormously, and that in a certain modest way he is an expert in a small field of study.

It is easy for him to forget that his reader has not come along with him, and it is tempting for him to assume that he can drop into the idiom of his topic and be clearly understood. Now this is a bad mistake. If he is not awake to his danger he will most certainly lose his clarity. That is, his reader will be lost from the start; he will never know where and when the essay begins and what its importance is in the wide field of human action. In fact the essay will be a little bundle of esoteric lore which demands of the reader much more foreknowledge than anyone has the right to demand.

The reader is no fool. If led by the hand through a slow and orderly introduction, if told about the general nature of the topic, if cajoled and humored, and told things he knew and has forgotten, he may gradually be pulled into the most complicated sort of explanation and follow it with ease and pleasure. When he enjoys this experience he will always say something about the clearness of the essay. In short, instruction number one in the achievement of clarity is: "Introduce your subject in a simple and general way; so orient it that almost any reader will be able to sense its importance." If this rule is obeyed the reader will be able to follow the argument into its complexities without any great pain. He will not feel himself swept into a new and incomprehensible world. The reading of the essay will be an interesting part of the continuousness of his mental life. In a certain large sense then, the clarity which emerges from a careful and gradual introduction is a clarity closely related to that other phenomenon, continuity.

The introduction *must not be too gradual*. That is, if the topic of the essay is the French Elections of 1837 the introduction should not start with the fall of the Roman Empire. This will come as a shock to some 10 per cent of undergraduate essay writers who conceive of the introduction as that gratifyingly thick batch of typed pages which carry the content of Freshman History. This is no introduction; the instructor who reads it will have another name for it.

There is a good deal more to be said about the matter of continuity within the essay proper. Briefly the admonition is this: the essay which is composed of words, phrases, sentences, paragraphs, sections, and chapters, must be fused into a unity by making these progressively complicated word structures lead to and flow into one another. The good writer contrives this flow largely by the observance of elemental rules, and these happily may be passed on in a certain rough form.

Everyone knows the virtue of gentle transition. It is a principle of kindliness and sympathy. It is as important in writing as it is in all other phases of life. People don't slam doors on unloved guests and don't shout "no" at unwanted solicitors. They edge the guests with firm but affable determination to the door, and they generally arrange to decline magazine subscriptions but decline them with polite decisiveness. They do the deed with a minimum of abruptness and a due consideration of the feelings of others. Good writing has this quality running through it from introduction to final summary. It is a web of ingratiating transitions between chapters, sections of chapters, paragraphs, and even sentences themselves.

Transitions are of two kinds; one we may name for Virginia Woolf who uses it to perfection and the other for Carl Becker who has preached and practiced it. The Woolf transition depends above all upon some slight connection in language. For example as often as not two important paragraphs are joined together by repeating a key word or phrase of the last sentence of the first paragraph in the opening sentence of the succeeding one. The reader spins from one to the other, borne by nothing more substantial than the word "time," or "woods," or "spring." The two paragraphs often have nothing else in common. They may not be bound to each other by thought, or subject, or the rules of logic, yet so compelling is the device that the reader passes from image to unrelated image without any sense of being gulled. If you are writing fiction and can use the Woolf transition like Woolf or Marcel Proust, use it and make a name. On the other hand if you are writing history, the Becker technique is more powerful and far more honest.

The proponents of the Becker school hold that if you cannot make a natural and unforced transition between two paragraphs, there is something wrong with your plan of presentation. They hold that there is an almost preordained order, which need not be strictly chronological or topical, but an order which is purely intellectual and is the inevitable product of the writer's mind. They feel that when he possesses a basketfull of related facts his mind can contrive a single best way of presenting them. And his highest duty to himself and his readers is to find that way. When he does find it, paragraph will lead to paragraph according to the inner sense of the text and not merely according to the deft placing of the trick word. The great historian ought to be followed by the lesser even if the going is rough.

Satisfactory chapters very often end with a paragraph which is dedicated to drawing the content together, summarizing it, and pointing the way to the next stage of the story. If the material has been difficult and closely reasoned, the reader will delight in a straightforward summary; if, on the other hand, the narrative has been an uncomplicated one, he will be bored by what he considers an unnecessary repetition. Not all chapters demand the transition paragraph. Those which do not are the ones in which the material may be molded throughout, sentence by sentence, to make the direction of meaning clear to the average reader.

For example, if one were writing about the British legislature and were discussing the broad powers of the House of Commons in chapter one, it would be a very easy matter to introduce from time to time a word or two about the House of Lords. It would be easy also to leave for last those powers of the Commons which were restricted by those of the upper house. If this were done the next chapter which dealt with the House of Lords would follow as a matter of course. On the other hand if the subject were a comparison of the upper houses of Great Britain and the United States the need for a transition paragraph might be greater. In such circumstances the reader might appreciate some word of summary at the end of the first chapter. And certainly he would better grasp the significance of chapter two in the essay as a whole if it were briefly introduced in this way.

Paragraphs themselves are little chapters, and the same general rules which govern the chapter should govern their construction. Their content should be introduced by what the rhetoric books call a topic sentence. Now this last is a statement which many a book on writing presents in just this form. The topic sentence is to the paragraph what the introduction was to the whole essay, and, to reduce the scale of comparison, it is what the introductory paragraph was to the chapter. Its function is one of lubrication. It smooths the way from paragraph to paragraph by binding that which has been said to that which is going to be said. By hooking the previous series of ideas to the coming one, it provides momentum.

The topic sentence is not always a single sentence; oftentimes it is a little bundle of two or three sentences. The space it eventually occupies in the paragraph must necessarily depend upon the complexity of the problem of transition. If the sense has been flowing in a simple and easily understood way, then paragraphs need a minimum of introducing. But when the going is hard, and the content is strange or closely reasoned, the writer can well afford to err on the side of over-introduction.

But don't introduce every paragraph with a formal topic sentence. Prose beaten out according to any rigid mechanical law will be dull and monotonous. Even the beginning writer can afford to take liberties with the topic sentence rule, if he bears its function in mind.

Within the paragraph the sentences ought to follow in logical order. This injunction should be no surprise to anyone. Come to think of it, almost any order may be defended as a logical one by the person who writes it. But in exposition the *reader* is the important person. Actually the aim in writing a sequence of sentences is not to be logical but to give the reader the feeling of inevitability. Contriving this inevitability of sequence is one of the most difficult parts of the whole writing business. A certain large amount of it may be done by using words of specific reference. "Therefore," "on the other hand," "moreover," "however," "to be sure," "no doubt," "it may be said," "indeed," and so on can be summoned and made to join the sense of two or three or four sentences. They force the reader's mind back over the preceding material and make it jump the small gaps over the punctuation. Repetition of the key word of one sentence in a second may perform this same service. President Roosevelt's radio speeches are models of tightly woven sentence structure. But whatever mechanical device be employed as a liaison, the beginner should realize that the best writers are able to get along with a bare minimum of these useful but unsubtle dodges. Richard Harding Davis, who had a good journalistic style, used to pack his original sentences with every conceivable connective device and then in second and third drafts see how many he could reasonably cut out. As he weeded he kept asking himself if the sense were still clear, and when he got to the danger point he stopped cutting.

Sometimes owing to the complexity of the subject matter, it becomes extremely difficult to arrange sentences within a paragraph so that they flow and still make sense. There are two ways of meeting this problem.

One of these demands that the writer write out his whole

argument on scratch paper in simple declarative sentences. No sentence may have in it more than one single simple idea. When the various ideas have thus been separated from one another, they become much easier to juggle, rearrange, and put in their right places. The writer may also see at a glance which of his ideas are of first importance and which of third or fourth. His concept of the structure of the paragraph may appear in a flash, and he will realize that a revision in the order of the simple declarative sentences will give him the sense and the clarity he desires and the particular sequence of ideas which he feels to be proper. At this moment he is ready to begin combining his simple sentences into more complicated ones. Some may turn out as compound or complex sentences, some in turn may shrink to simple adjectives or adverbs. The following is an example: "There was a man without any hat on whose clothes were badly torn and who was running in an obvious hurry down the street to catch a bus which did not wait for him, and so he missed it." [4] This may be broken down into these simple declarative sentences:

> There was a man.
> The man wore a suit.
> The suit was badly torn.
> The man had no hat.
> The man was running.
> He was in a hurry.
> This was obvious.
> He wanted to catch the bus.
> The bus did not wait.
> The man missed the bus.

These sentences may now be combined into: "Hatless, his suit in tatters, a man vainly chased the bus. It did not wait." This example is obviously oversimplified, but it may illustrate

4. In case a student thinks that such an awkward phrasing is unlikely to be found in the prose works of college seniors, let him but ask one of his teachers about the literacy of his classmates.

the way in which relatively complicated ideas may be broken down into simple components and then recombined in clear and straightforward sentences.[5]

The second trick which will help clarify complex subject matter is one that most undergraduates know far too much about already. Vulgarly it may be called "padding," elegantly it may be termed "slowing down the pace of the narrative." It should be used only when the subject is both complex and closely reasoned. Suppose that you were asked to write a proposition from Euclid in paragraph form. Seemingly you could put each step of the theorem, if not two or three of them, into a single sentence. In any case the resultant paragraph would be composed of sentences whose content was too concentrated for the mind to grasp. The eyes, accustomed to move rapidly from one sentence to the next, might well be reading the third sentence before the mind had taken in the first. This being the case, the paragraph would convey very little sense, and the reader would have to go back and reread it two or three times. It is not too much to ask this of the reader, but he should be spared as much of it as possible. And he may be spared it, if the writer, realizing his difficulty, will be so kind as to slow up the narrative in those places where the going is tough. This he can do by writing two sentences where one sufficed in the original, by saying the same thing a second time in different words. This device is dangerous, for if it is used where not vitally necessary the reader will be bored, not to say insulted.

So much for the positive means of achieving a continuity and clarity of narrative. Before I drop the whole subject the student ought to have another bit of advice upon the negative aspect of the problem—how to avoid discontinuity. For it is not enough

5. On this highly technical problem of constructing sentences and paragraphs see Joseph M. Thomas and others, eds., *Composition for College Students* (N.Y., 1937), Chapter III, esp. pp. 147–153.

that he take the preceding advice to heart and observe it, he should also be warned of another group of "don'ts."

The first of these is the unwarranted use of quotation. Very often a student doing his first piece of serious writing and feeling the weight of his inexperience will try to give his essay a false maturity by elaborate quotation from his reading. He should not do this for a few sound reasons. To begin with, the practice is founded in an unbecoming disingenuousness which he most emphatically should not cultivate. He did not come to college to learn how to bluff. In the second place unless quotation is most skillfully used and the quoted passage woven into the narrative with great nicety, it obstructs the flow of the argument. In the third place there are very few things worth a verbatim quotation.

Passages from textbooks and general secondary works should never be quoted, unless the words themselves are to be the subject of a careful analysis. The content of most such books is duplicated in a hundred others, and the risk of destroying continuity does not make exact quotation worthwhile. Passages from the monographs of the master historians should not be quoted unless they are so trenchant that they add to the impressiveness of the argument. Just because Maitland, or Ranke, or Fustel said it, is no reason in itself for carrying it over into a new manuscript. Above all do not quote in a foreign language. There is no sense in assuming that the reader is able to understand the language. Furthermore, no matter how well he reads it, he will find that changing from one speech to another disturbs his stream of consciousness even more than moving from one style to another within his own language. He will tend to skip over the quotation. If the quoted words are important in the flow of meaning, the pardonably lazy reader will promptly lose the sense. Generally speaking, students intrude foreign phrases into their essays to make a bold show of their erudition or be-

cause they cannot translate the passages themselves. Neither of these is valid reason to disturb the reader's equanimity.[6]

Admittedly there are expressions in foreign languages which are so good in themselves and so meager when given an English equivalent that they should be left in the original. There are also expressions that defy a literal English translation. When you come upon one of these you should put it into workmanlike English, taking any liberties you feel necessary, and bolster your translation by exactly quoting the original in a footnote.[7] This will assure you a minimal disturbance in the sequence of the argument.

However hard you try to avoid quotation, there are times when it is extremely useful, even essential. Sometimes it is mandatory for the sense or forcefulness of the argument, sometimes it is the main point of departure for a long and important analysis, and sometimes it is too good a thing to be tampered with. In such circumstances quote, and quote with a clear conscience. Try, however, to make the quotation a part of your own work; introduce it in your own words; substitute your own paraphrase when it becomes prolix; steel yourself to junking the best passage unless it is relevant; chop up the rest, use what you want, and throw away the remains. There is no reason to perpetuate

6. Every once in a while a student who insists on quoting widely in a foreign tongue will say in a footnote, "I am not translating this material because to do so would spoil the purity of its meaning." He then proceeds to rape the vaunted purity by leaving out accents, putting wrong endings on the verbs, dropping an occasional word, and mixing genders. His reader's criticism is apt to be cruel and justifiably so. If the student must quote in another's language, he ought to do it accurately.

7. One last word about another use of quotation marks. Sometimes the student will want to use an expression which is slangy or odd or colloquial and will not want to take full responsibility for it. He calls upon the quotation mark to prove to his reader that he knows that the expression sounds "fromagenous." This is an unimaginative if not cowardly way to meet the situation. If he is afraid of the expression and does not want to claim authorship, he should substitute another for which he is willing to take the rap.

incoherent or banal remarks even though a great man wrote them. But whatever you do to the quotation, be scrupulously sure that you keep to the original sense. Like this:

In his magnificent speeches for the Reform Bill Macaulay thundered, "I believe it is possible to obtain some insight into the law which regulates the growth of communities, and some knowledge of the effects which that growth produces. . . . God has decreed that old age shall succeed to manhood and manhood to infancy. *Even so have societies their laws of growth.*[8] " Obstruct the working of these laws and observe the terrible exactions which time will take. Gracious Parisian *hôtels* are now lodging houses, and lovely *châteaux* lie in ruins because the aristocracy of France was purblind. ". . . [because] it resisted reform in 1783, it was unable to resist revolution in 1789. . . . [because] it would not endure Turgot . . . it had to endure Robespierre."

Another menace to the continuity of the essay is irrelevancy. Irrelevant material may be of two main sorts: material which has no direct relation to the subject; material which has a remote relation to the subject, but which is improperly overemphasized. To escape from the morass of the first, the student needs nothing beyond courage and a red pencil. A frank analysis of his essay and a sentence-by-sentence hunt for expressions which do not forward the narrative is all that he requires (besides the pencil) to rid his work of disconcerting digression.

The second sort of irrelevancy is much more difficult to cut away. Basically it is not so much a question of irrelevancy as it is one of emphasis and under this heading the rhetoric books usually discuss it. Briefly it may be illustrated by going back to the essay outlined at the beginning of this chapter. The student, it will be recalled, was writing on an election and had decided that the title of the essay was *The Election of 1837 in France.* The title obviously called for a certain pattern of presentation; and when the reader first saw the title he may well have assumed that the author would follow an arrangement like the one

8. Italics mine.

suggested in the sample outline. He expected to read an account of the two contesting parties and an analysis of the result of the contest. The writer having promised some such discussion in both title and introduction must abide by his word.

When a well-intentioned writer breaks this promise he does it most frequently by an improper distribution of emphasis. Let us say the writer told his reader he was going to describe this election of 1837. Let us say that when he advanced to the point of describing the campaign of the "Outs" that he found a great deal of interesting material. So large in bulk was it and so diverting to him that he wrote at great length about it. He went from campaign, to party organization, to party leaders, to their political attributes, to their economic status, to their families, and thence to their wives' families. Let us say that he did not find similar material on the "In" group, and in consequence his treatment of it was skimpy. Now it is comparatively useless to point out that the essay which purports to be a description of a campaign is ill-conceived if the emphasis is distributed in this fashion. To overemphasize the "Out" party is tantamount to including irrelevant material in connection with it. With this material left in, the essay will be far from satisfactory.

What will the author do in this situation? First, he may change the title and introduction of the essay; call it *The Opposition in the French Election of 1837;* and cut out all the material relating to the "In" party. This course of action will be feasible only where the topic was too broad a one to begin with. Or he may deftly prune away most of the material relating to the "Outs" which he cannot match for the "Ins." Thirdly, he may grind this extra material down and use the more interesting and relevant bits as illustrative footnotes. Here it will appear outside the main narrative and undisturbing of the narrative's proper emphasis. Here it will be at the disposal of the interested reader who may take it or leave it as he pleases. The proper uses of the footnote are told in the next chapter.

One last suggestion. No one can expect to write a finished essay in a single draft, and no one (except the green beginner or the newspaperman who is short of time) ever tries. Although students have been told the virtues of second and third drafts from the time they learned to write, they are still reluctant to take the trouble. The results are scandalous. Sentences don't parse; verbs are written in the wrong person and tense; the style is jerky; the order disconcerting; very frequently even the sense is gone. The only way to iron out a manuscript is to reread it (read it aloud if possible), correct it, revise it, and rewrite it. Don't ask your teachers to read something which is not your most careful and workmanlike job. There is enough of the craftsman in everyone to make the doing of precise and finished work its own satisfying reward.

# CHAPTER VI

# Style and Usage

## I. GENERAL REMARKS ON STYLE AND USAGE

That the serious essay deal with a proper subject, and that its unfolding compel the attention of the earnest reader is not enough. In addition it ought to have a professional appearance which will shout the academic maturity of its author. This professional appearance emerges as the result of obedience to one single injunction: *accepted and consistent usage.* If the student can force himself to be consistent in the matters of footnoting and citation, spelling and punctuation, quotation, numbers and dates, capitalization, compounding, and italics, he will not only be putting himself through an exercise of great disciplinary value, but will also be giving a self-respecting appearance to his writing. Or to put the matter on a far baser level, it may be said that readers who are obliged by college requirements to grade essays, will oftentimes tend to overestimate the quality of one which employs a consistent usage. Very frequently the loving care which this quality seems to symbolize turns out to be (in the reader's opinion) the very significant difference between pass and failure or A plus and A minus.

However important the matter of correct usage, it can become a nonsensical obsession. Since all important metropolitan newspapers, respectable magazines, and large publishing houses have their own style books, and since no two of these texts are in anything like complete agreement, the chance for debate over questions like the abbreviation of captain (capt. with the period, because the abbreviation does not end in the same letter as the word) and lieutenant (lieut without the period, because the abbreviation does end in the same letter) are eternal, not to say a little ridiculous. The rules about to be set forth are as simplified as may be, and as is quite obvious they are not sacrosanct. The student might just as well accept the dictates of the Oxford Press, the Yale Press, or the University of Chicago Press. No matter which he accepts, the reader of his essay will demand that they be employed with *accuracy* and *clarity* and *consistency*.

## II. PHYSICAL APPEARANCE OF THE PAPER

The essay should have a title page. The title, the student's name, and the date should be typed in capitals. The essay itself should be typed double-space on only one side of the paper.

Ordinary stenographic rules for spacing, margins, indentations, should prevail.

Footnotes and references should appear in single-space and should be separated from the text by a line, a broken line, or some other device. Footnotes may be numbered consecutively within each page, but if the manuscript is to be printed the notes run consecutively throughout the section or chapter. If there are more than one hundred notes, the hundred and first may be numbered as "1," the hundred and second as "2," etc.[1]

In a relatively short paper, it is a little ostentatious to dignify eight or ten pages of typescript with the name chapter. For the

---

1. If you are typing your manuscript for publication, footnotes should appear either at the bottom of each page, or all together on a separate group of sheets at the end of the chapter. Printers rather prefer this second method. Putting your notes together this way *does not* mean that they will appear thus in print. They can be (and usually are) placed at the bottom of the proper pages.

moment at least call these groups of pages "sections" and indicate the break between them by a blank line or two; use a roman numeral if the break is a profound one. Reserve the word chapter for the major divisions (divisions of twenty to thirty pages) of longer papers (papers which reach eighty to a hundred pages or more). Start each chapter on a new sheet, give it its proper number (in Roman numerals), and a title.

Appendices and the bibliographical note should be double-spaced and should begin on fresh sheets.[2]

*Proofread the manuscript with care.* Do not rely upon your own or a professional's typing. Make corrections in ink and make them as neatly as possible.

## III. FOOTNOTES

Footnotes are of two sorts; the one serves to illuminate or supplement the text by explaining it, the other to validate the text by citing an authority. The first is a footnote proper, the second a citation or reference note. Although both often appear in the same note, as they should, let us discuss them separately.

### A. THE FOOTNOTE PROPER

As explained at the end of the last chapter, use the footnote proper as a device to bring material into the manuscript which bears upon the subject of the text, which is interesting in itself, yet which is not sufficiently relevant to the text to be incorporated in it. The note should be composed with economy; its substance should be compact. It should not be so long as to dominate the page; very definitely it should be too short to appear as an appendix. For example: If the essay were dealing with the tactics of Waterloo, and if the writer discovered on

2. The appendix and the bibliographical note are discussed on pp. 98, 99–101.

impeccable authority that on that day Napoleon was suffering from one of his intolerable headaches, and considered this sufficiently interesting and germane, let him put it into a note. Typed in single-space it could be as long as one hundred words, possibly longer. If it demanded three or four hundred words, it should go into an appendix—that is, if it were worth three or four hundred words to begin with.

On the other hand, if the student were making the point that Napoleon's tactics on the day of Waterloo were those of a man with a desperate headache and if the headache was a significant part of his argument, then the substance of the note does not belong in a note at all, but rather in the text where it is necessary for the general argument.

Use the foot*note* proper also for such purposes as:

1. Giving the modern American equivalent of unfamiliar weights and measures: *carucate*, about 120 acres; *hectare*, 2.7 acres; *quarter*, about 8 bushels; *rupee*, 32.44 cents in pre–1933 exchange, but not the *pound sterling* or the *Reichsmark* unless the exchange rate is of formal importance.

2. Explaining fully the technical meaning of a word borrowed from another language and used in the text for reasons of economy: *cens*, the sum of money paid in direct taxes necessary to confer the franchise upon the payer. After such an explanation it will be possible to refer to the word *cens* without further definition. However if a large part of the text will be devoted to the subject of the *cens*, obviously the term should be defined in the text.

3. Giving the original of a passage quoted from a foreign language, particularly when the textual translation has been slangy, colloquial, or loose.

4. Setting forth the two sides of a minor controversial point; illustrating a complicated heritage by means of a family tree; offering statistical or tabular material which is hard to write out,

and the conclusions from which have already appeared in the text.

A last word, and a general one, about footnotes. Do not overwork them; do not mistake pedantry for scholarship.

## B. THE CITATION OR REFERENCE NOTE

Many of the statements made in the text demand validation. The reader has the right to ask, "Where did he get that?" and the writer has the obligation to answer. The reader however will not question all the statements. The parts of the essay he will especially wish to have footnoted are these: (1) all direct quotations, unless obviously familiar; (2) quotations and paraphrases of documents or passages from sources, monographs, and other secondary work; (3) statistical material such as trade figures, population figures, debt figures, and the like; (4) iconoclastic remarks, statements which deny a legend, which deflate a widely-accepted generalization, statements which at first blush seem improbable; (5) new ideas from the sources not found in the texts and monographs; (6) specific statements from newspapers particularly when used as evidence of opinion. The writer must explain where he found these things and to do so habitually employs the citation or reference note.

General advice: Do not cite from textbooks unless the wording itself is up for debate. Facts of common knowledge such as the date of Waterloo or the Declaration of Independence need no citation. Famous remarks like, "I only regret that I have but one life to lose for my country," need no citation; nor do rough population figures of an important nation in an era of accurate censuses. If the terms of a well-known treaty or agreement are generalized, there is no necessity to quote the authority, but if the exact wording of the text of such a treaty is important in the narrative, then the locus of the document should be made known. The same rule would obtain in the matter of constitutions, statutes, and other documents of state.

When a citation or footnote is explanatory of a particular word or phrase, the figure [3] which indicates the note in the text should follow the word or the phrase; otherwise this figure should come at the end of the sentence or whole passage to which the note refers. This is especially important when a document is being paraphrased and doubt might arise as to when the paraphrasing ends and the general discussion resumes.[4]

## 1. Forms for Citations

There are two main sorts of material (unpublished and published) which are usually cited in footnotes of historical writing. Each has its own particular reference form. In the interest of consistency in usage it is important that the student be able to cite them in the accepted professional manner. Proper citation is largely a matter of correct capitalization, punctuation, use of italics (underscoring in the typescript), and use of quotation marks, and the student should study the following examples and try to use them consistently.

### a. *Unpublished Manuscript Material*

Citation of unpublished material in general demands neither italics nor quotation marks. Since such material is unique, information on the geographical situs of private or little-known collections is very valuable. Specific dates and identifying names, wherever possible, should be given. The words— "papers," "diary," "manuscript," or "manuscripts" (abbreviated MS. and MSS.), "collection," and "correspondence"— should be used in accordance with the practice of the repository.

---

3. [Thus] Printers call this the superior figure.
4. [Thus] This paragraph is quoted almost verbatim from L. W. Labaree, *Notes on the Preparation of Historical Papers* (Mimeographed and privately circulated), p. 3.

### (1) MANUSCRIPT COLLECTIONS [5]

Example:
George B. McClellan to Samuel McClellan, Sept. 27, 1864, Library of Congress, George B. McClellan Papers.

If documents from such a collection are to be cited many times the following short cut to full citation may be adopted:

First reference:
George B. McClellan to Samuel McClellan, Sept. 27, 1864, Library of Congress, George B. McClellan Papers. Hereafter cited as McClellan Papers.

Next reference:
G. B. McClellan to S. McClellan, Sept. 30, 1864, McClellan Papers.

### (2) DIARIES, JOURNALS AND LETTERBOOKS

Examples:
Entry of Feb. 20, 1916, Diary of Edward M. House, MS. in the House Collection of the Yale University Library. Hereafter cited as House Diary.

The True Yankee Boy, MS. in Yale University Library, composition signed by Mr. Locomotive, Feb. 25, 1835. Hereafter cited as Yankee Boy MS.

Journal of Winthrop Sargent, Oct. 1, 1793–Dec. 31, 1795 (typed copy in Ohio State Archaeological and Historical Society), pp. 41–62. Hereafter cited as Sargent Journal.

### (3) ARCHIVAL MATERIAL

American example:
Deposition of Edward Ward, June 30, 1756, Ohio Co. Papers, I, 10, Library of the Historical Society of Pennsylvania, Philadelphia. Hereafter cited as Ohio Co. Papers.

5. For many of the suggestions on the citation of manuscript material I am indebted to Miss Bertha E. Josephson, Editorial Associate of the *Mississippi Valley Historical Review*. Miss Josephson is herself preparing a style manual for historical publications which will be much more complete than this short chapter.

Foreign examples—England:
  Memorandum of Captain Elliot's conference with Kishen, 31
  Aug., 1840, India Office, China Correspondence, X. Hereafter
  cited abbreviated, I.O., China Corresp.
  Petition of Samuel Briggs, Feb. 8, 1806, Public Record Office,
  Egypt, 24:2, pp. 5–7. Hereafter abbreviated as P.R.O., Egypt.

Foreign examples—France:
  Minister of the interior to prefect of the Marne, Sept. 5, 1835,
  Archives Nationales, Esprit public et élections $F^{1c111}$ Marne 5.
  Hereafter cited as A.N. $F^{1c111}$ Marne 5.

## b. *Published or Printed Material*

### (1) GENERAL REMARKS

(a) *Fugitives*. The citation of published material, whether
in documentary or other form, demands the proper use of
quotation marks and italics (underscoring in typescript). Since
such material is apt to be available in many libraries it is seldom
necessary to tell where it may be found. However in the case of
unique copies, fugitives, and other bibliographical rarities,
reference to the library which owns them may be exceedingly
useful.

Example:
  Anon., *The Hystory of the Valyaunt Bretheren Valentine and
  Orson* (London, [1565?]), pp. 10–12. Unique perfect copy in
  the Yale University Library.

(b) *Use of italics*. In the footnote citation of printed and
published books and pamphlets, the title is always italicized.[6]

6. The rules for punctuating titles, etc., which follow are in the main
good for both reference notes and the bibliographical essay. One exception:
In a reference note it is not mandatory to tell the number of volumes of a
given work—even at the first mention. In the bibliographical essay it *is*
essential to tell the number of volumes. If the bibliography *is not written
in the form of an essay*, but is simply a list of titles (which is very poor custom
these days), the entries may be made in a different style. Like this: Donald
C. McKay, *The National Workshops*. Cambridge (Mass), 1933. Or: Paul
Thureau-Dangin, *Histoire de la monarchie de juillet*. 7 vols., Paris, 1882–91.

The general rule is to use italics for the material presented on the book's title page. The author's name of course is printed in Roman. Thus: Douglas K. Reading, *The Anglo-Russian Commercial Treaty of 1734* (New Haven, 1938), pp. 16–25. And when the citation is from a journal or collaborative work, the same practice holds. Thus: Michael I. Rostovtzeff, "The Hellenistic World and Its Economic Development," *American Historical Review*, vol. 41 (1935–36), 246.[7] Notice that the name of the journal, which does appear on the title page, is italicized while the title of the article, which does not (at least in the bound volume), is set off in quotation marks. Notice also in the case of a collaborative work: George M. Trevelyan, "The Age of Johnson," in A. S. Turberville, ed., *Johnson's England* (Oxford, 1933), I, 9–10.

(c) *Capitalization within a cited title:*

### For books in English

Capitalize: (1) The first word
(2) All other words except articles, conjunctions, and prepositions.

Examples:
*The Balance of Power.*
*Iron and Steel in the Industrial Revolution.*
*An Estimate of the Comparative Strength of Great Britain during the Present and Four Preceding Reigns.*
*The War behind the War.*

### For books in German

Capitalize: (1) The first word
(2) All nouns and proper nouns, all compounded words which carry a substantive sense.

Note: Do *not* capitalize adjectives even though they are derived from proper nouns: *Die französische Frage, Die friedericianische*

7. If the article is cited in its entirety it is considered proper to put in the pages which it occupies. Thus: *American Historical Review*, vol. 41 (1935–36), 231–252. But for the citation of a specific something on a given page or pages use the above form.

*Politik.* But when the adjective is actually the genitive case of a proper noun it should be capitalized: *Der Kölner Dom,* but *Die kölnischen Zeitungen.*

Examples:
*Krieg und Kriegführung im Wandel der Weltgeschichte.*
*Geschichte der friedericianischen Politik.*
*Die neueste Geschichte des jüdischen Volkes.*

### For books in French

Capitalize: [8] (1) The first word
            (2) All proper nouns
Note: Do *not* capitalize any adjective, whether or not derived from a proper noun.

Examples:
*Mémoires d'un bourgeois de Paris.*
*Les clubs de Barbès et de Blanqui.*
*La question allemande.*
*Elections et élus.* (Note that capital letters need not be accented
  —*élus* but *Elus.*)

(d) *Form and punctuation of the cited book—first reference.* The first words of the citation are the author's name, written as it appears on the title page, followed by a comma. Then should follow in italics the complete title, as it appears on the title page (not as it appears on the binding). Then without any other punctuation mark follows the opening half of a parenthesis. Then comes the edition you are citing (if neces-

8. There is an alternative scheme of capitalization which is widely used and which may be substituted for the one above. It is not preferred usage.
Capitalize: (1) The first word
           (2) The first substantive
           (3) All proper nouns
Note: When the first word is also the first substantive do not capitalize anything else in the title except proper nouns. Do not capitalize any adjective as above.
Examples:
*Les Clubs de Barbès et de Blanqui.*
*L'abominable Vénalité de la presse française.*
*Mémoires d'un bourgeois de Paris.*

sary to mention this), followed by a comma, then the number of volumes, if you choose, then a comma. Then follow place of publication, comma, date or dates of publication, closing half of parenthesis, comma. Then follow the volume (if a multi-volume work), comma and page reference, period. Here is the end of most full citations.

If the date of the first edition of the work is important it comes after the last period: 1st ed., 1896.

Examples:
> Donald C. McKay, *The National Workshops* (Cambridge, Mass., 1933), pp. 155–156.
> Paul Thureau-Dangin, *Histoire de la monarchie de juillet* (Paris, 1882–92 [9]), VI, 227–234.

Notice that the page reference in a single-volume work demands the abbreviation p. or pp. before the page number, and that in a multivolume work the abbreviations vol. or vols., p. or pp. are *not* used. The volume number in a multivolume work is always written in Roman numerals,[10] the page numbers in Arabic.

(e) *Anonymous books.* If a book or pamphlet is published anonymously, the fact can oftentimes be noted in the text, in which case the footnote need have no mention of it. But if for any reason this cannot be contrived, an anonymous work should be cited thus: Anon., *The Life of the Bee.* Where the place and date of publication is also lacking this may be indicated

9. In dating a work published over two or more years do not repeat the number of the century in the second year: 1882–92, *not* 1882–1892. If the two dates span the turn of a century naturally both century numbers must be included: 1892–1901.

10. Do not use Roman numerals for volume numbers when the numeral will be long and complicated. For instance to cite CLXXIX of the *Patrologia Latina* would be a dubious favor to your reader. Vol. 179 would be much kinder. To be arbitrary, start making your numbers Arabic at 40, and when you use them precede them with the abbreviation "vol." to keep your reader from thinking that you are talking of pages.

with the abbreviations n.p.[11] and n.d. (no place of publication, no date). Thus: Anon., *The Life of the Bee* (n.p., n.d.), p. 17. If an undated book can be dated by other evidence than what appears on the title page, the date or approximate date should be given in square brackets. Thus: Sam Raul, *Ticker Tape* (N.Y., [1930]), p. 20. Or Sam Raul, *Ticker Tape* (n.p., [c. 1930]), p. 20.

(f) *Repeated citation of the same book.* If a book or article is to be cited over and over again, it ought not to be cited in its entirety on each occasion. Some authors meet the demands of repeated citation by using the Latin abbreviations *op. cit.* and *loc. cit.* Oftentimes the use of these is extremely confusing, and the following technique is considered preferable. At the first reference the work is cited in full, with an explanation of the short title to be used subsequently. Thus: Ray S. Baker, *Woodrow Wilson and World Settlement* (N.Y., 1922), II, 167. Hereafter cited as R. S. Baker, *World Settlement*. Subsequent references then merely use the shortened title: R. S. Baker, *World Settlement* with the proper volume and page reference.

However not all citations demand this ceremony. Some books when cited in abbreviated form are still unmistakable, and the short title does not demand the heralding "hereafter cited as." For example, if the first reference was: Hermann A. Keyserling, *The Travel Diary of a Philosopher* (N.Y., 1925; trans. J. Holroyd Reece), pp. 25–35, a later reference to H. A. Keyserling, *Diary*, would be perfectly clear.

Always identify the author by giving his first name or initials. Do not cite Smith, *A History of Modern Culture*, or Smith, *Parties and Slavery*. Cite them as Preserved Smith, *Modern Culture*; and T. C. Smith, *Parties and Slavery*.

---

11. Some books or pamphlets are not paginated, and when an author cites one of these creations of idiocy, he sometimes uses the abbreviation n.p. to mean no numbered pages. A small amount of ingenuity on his part can prevent any confusion over the two possible meanings.

## (2) CORRECT FORMS OF CITATION

(a) *First citation of a single or multivolume work by a single author:* Harry R. Rudin, *Germans in the Cameroons, 1884–1914* (New Haven, 1938), pp. 150–161. Sidney B. Fay, *The Origins of the World War* (N.Y., 1928), I, 116–124; II, 15–20.

(b) *First citation of a single or multivolume work by two authors:* Charles Gide and Charles Rist, *A History of Economic Doctrine* (Boston [1932], trans. by R. Richards), pp. 208–209. Hereafter cited as C. Gide and C. Rist, *Economic Doctrine*. Samuel E. Morison and Henry S. Commager, *The Growth of the American Republic* (N.Y., 1937), II, 18–25.

If more than two authors co-operate on a work, give the full name of the first to appear on the title page, and follow it by "and others"; see the example used for editors on this page.

(c) *First citation of a single or multivolume work edited by a single editor:* Margaret Spahr, ed., *Readings in Recent Political Philosophy* (N.Y., 1935), p. 64. Hereafter cited as M. Spahr, *Readings*. Charles Seymour, ed., *The Intimate Papers of Colonel House* (Boston, 1926–28), II, 156–175. Hereafter cited as C. Seymour, *House Papers*.

(d) *First citation of a single or multivolume work edited by two editors and by more than two editors:* William H. Dunham Jr. and Stanley Pargellis, eds., *Complaint and Reform in England* (N.Y., 1938), p. 65. When there are more than two editors, use the following device: George M. Dutcher and others, eds., *A Guide to Historical Literature* (N.Y., 1931), p. 50. Lord Acton and others, eds., *The Cambridge Modern History* (Reprinted N.Y., 1934), X, 150–175.

(e) *First citation of a section or chapter of a collaborative work edited by one or more editors:* H. L. Beales, "Travel and Communications," in A. S. Turberville, ed., *Johnson's England* (Oxford, 1933), I, 123–159. Hereafter cited as H. L. Beales, "Travel." F. Meinecke, "Liberalism and Nationality in Germany and Austria (1840–48)" in Lord Acton and others, eds., *The Cambridge Modern History* (N.Y., 1934), XI, 43. Hereafter cited as F. Meinecke, "Liberalism and Nationality."

(f) *Citation of almanacs, registers, year books: The World Almanac* (N.Y., 1934), pp. 208–210. *The Annual Register* (London, 1936), pp. 198–199. *Who's Who in America* (N.Y., 1939). *The Statesman's Year Book* (London, 1930), pp. 140–146.

(g) *First citation of signed articles in magazines and journals, transactions, proceedings, publications, reports, collections, and the like:* R. A. Winnacker, "The Third French Republic," *Journal of Modern History*,[12] X (1938), pp. 372–409. Margaret Lafever, "Story of Early Life in Michigan," Michigan Pioneer and Historical Society, *Collections*, XXXVIII (1912), 673. Frederick J. Turner, "The Significance of the Frontier in American History," American Historical Association, *Annual Report*, 1893 (Washington, 1894). Notice that only the words "Collections," "Annual Report," "Proceedings," "Digests," and the like in such publications are italicized.

(h) *Citation of important signed articles in encyclopedias and biographical dictionaries:* As a general rule the simple citation of the article and the work is sufficient. Thus: "France," *Encyclopedia Britannica* (11th ed.). However there are contributions to these large works which are as important for their authorship as for their content, and these deserve a fuller citation. Thus: T. E. Lawrence, "Guerilla Warfare," *Encyclopedia Britannica* (14th ed.).

(i) *Citation from newspapers:* Do not italicize the name of the city if it is part of the paper's title. New York *Times*,[13]

12. The real title of this journal, if you look it up, is: *The Journal of Modern History*. Notice that the "The" is left off in the citation. So is it left off about every other similar title: N.Y. *Times*, not The N.Y. *Times*. In the text if you want to speak of the New York *Times*, do it without capitalizing the "the."

13. See note 10.

Apr. 27, 1938. Chicago *Tribune*, Apr. 28, 1902. If the town is small and not well known, the state should be mentioned. San Rafael (California) *Independent*, Dec. 1, 1903. If the paper does not bear the name of an identifying city italicize the whole title: *Daily Worker*, Aug. 26, 1939. Locate obscure papers with the city of publication and state if necessary: *Silver State Journal* (Winnemucca, Nev.), Dec. 6, 1890. *La Progrès du Pas de Calais* (Arras), Apr. 8, 1834.


# IV. SUGGESTIONS FOR CONSISTENCY IN USAGE

## A. CAPITALIZATION [14]

Modern usage in scholarly writing tends to steer away from capitalization, and the most helpful general rule to the writer is therefore, "Use as few caps as you dare." This is peculiarly good advice since the normal tendency of any writer (e.e. cummings excepted) is to overwork the big letters. Once he has made a single slip on the side of overcapitalization, the drive of logic will prevail over good taste (or good sense), and he will find his typed or printed page resembling a slice of Carlyle or Ezra Pound.

There are, however, a few things which must be capitalized.

### 1. Historical Events and Movements

The names of historical events and movements, like the Renaissance, the Counter-Reformation, the Battle of Gettysburg,[15] the French Revolution, the Restoration, are capitalized.

14. See for further detailed rules, *A Manual of Style . . . Used at the University of Chicago Press* (10th ed., Chicago, 1938), pp. 23–42. Hereafter cited as *Chicago Style Book*.

15. If you are writing military history and if your pages become crowded with the names of battles, large and small, it is preferable to drop them all to lower-case importance rather than to fill your page with caps.

## 2. Geographical Terms

Certain geographical expressions, like the North, *Nord*, the South, *Midi*, Northwest, are capitalized when referring to parts of a country or continent. These words must also be capitalized when they are part of a compound, like North America, Central Africa, South Carolina. They are *not* capitalized when used simply as points of the compass: southern France, the north of China. But, the South was defeated at Vicksburg.

Words like river, valley, mountains, gap, are capitalized when they are part of a specific geographical name: the Ohio River, the Sacramento Valley, the Sierra-Nevada Mountains, Cumberland Gap. But they are *not* capitalized when they are used in the plural, or when their sense is generic: the Ohio and Mississippi rivers, the Sacramento and San Joaquin valleys, the river of time, the mountains of southern Pennsylvania.

## 3. Titles

In certain personal titles capitalize all words except pronouns, articles, and prepositions: Duke of the Abruzzi, their Royal Highnesses; but in French and German: Son Altesse Royale, and Ihre Königlichen Hohheiten.

## 4. Government Officers and Organs

For officers and organs of government no general rule can be laid down. But be it said that the safe course is to overuse the small letters (lower case). For if one begins a description of the governmental pyramid and capitalizes presidency, logic will ineluctably lead to the capitalization of policeman and streetsweeper. By the same token it is dangerously easy to slip from capitalizing Parliament to speaker, to debate, down to remarks, down to town meeting and other things which manifestly belong in the lower case.

## 5. Political Terms

Certain words from the realm of politics, such as Constitution, State, Federal, Supreme Court, President, and the like, are capitalized when they relate to a specific American governmental institution. Capitalize them and all official titles when they are followed by the name of a person or state: President Roosevelt, the State of Nevada, the Federal Constitution of the United States, Secretary of State Hull, Chief Justice Hughes, Prime Minister Churchill, King George VI. Do *not* capitalize these titles when they are *not* followed by names: the secretary of labor, the king, the premier, the president of the council. Notice also, Cordell Hull, secretary of state, but Franklin D. Roosevelt, President of the United States. The word state when used as an abstraction is always lower case: the French state.[16] But it is capitalized when it appears in the expression Church and State.

## 6. Words Capitalized out of Respect

Certain words, out of respect, the names of the deity and pronouns relative to the deity, words of ritualistic significance: the Sacraments, Mass; also the words Catholic and Protestant; and words for races of mankind: the Caucasian, the Negroes, and Negro.

## B. Compounding

The problem of what words to write as one, what words to hyphenate, and what words to leave untied to one another is an exceedingly difficult one. Webster's dictionary represents standard American usage in the matter and should be used whenever there is a doubt. There are however a few main rules which dispose of some of the most frequent questions.

16. Note however: New York State, the Keystone State, the Nutmeg State, etc.

## 1. Co-, Pre-, Re-

Hyphenate when co-, pre-, re-, etc., are prefixed to words beginning with the vowel of the prefix, or when the prefix is followed by another vowel which would form a diphthong or otherwise cause confusion: co-operate, pre-empt, re-enter. The hyphen, which is nearly always used in *typescript* for obvious mechanical reasons, is Webster's *preferred usage even in print.* Many publishers follow Webster and do not employ the diaeresis (two dots over the second vowel: coöperate). The diaeresis is still in good repute however.

Check with Webster about hyphenating after prefixes like "non," "quasi," "anti," "ultra," "well," "self," "vice," and "pan." Modern usage is tending away from the hyphen more and more, particularly with respect to these prefixes. There is another equally strong tendency to run together words like newspaperman and even newspaperwoman.

## 2. Two Nouns

Hyphenate when the first word of a compound noun is the object of the second: harness-maker. This rule however is broken almost as often as maintained, for example: officeholder and landowner. When in doubt consult Webster.

## 3. Two or More Adjectival Modifiers

Hyphenate adjectives formed by two or more words when they *precede* the noun they modify: so-called Croesus, first-class investment, four-year-old boy. Notice especially: seventeenth-century England, but: The seventeenth century was an age of genius.

## 4. Other Compounds

Note that compounds which begin with an adverb ending in "ly" do not command a hyphen: a badly managed bank. Note

also that "a well-known character" is correct, but "He is a
character who is well known" calls for *no* hyphen.

### 5. Whole Cardinal Numbers

Hyphenate whole compound cardinal numbers: thirty-two,
twenty-six. Hyphenate cardinal numbers and their fractions
when they precede the noun they modify: four-and-a-quarter
pies, two-and-one-half years. But do not hyphenate the frac-
tional part of the number when the whole numerical expression
is used as a noun: His score was twenty-six and a half.

### 6. Hyphen, En–Dash, Em—Dash

Printers differentiate between the hyphen -, the en-dash –,
and the em-dash —, and use each for a different purpose. If you
are preparing a manuscript for press, it will be necessary to go
into these distinctions with considerable care.

### C. NUMBERS

Spell out in the text numbers less than one hundred, and even
hundreds up to one thousand, even tens of thousands, and hundreds of thousands, and so on: fifty-seven, ninety, one hundred,
fifty thousand; but 256, 51,000, and 4,750.[17] However, if the
numbers are part of a statistical series, appearing in the text do
*not* spell them out. Write them as numbers. Furthermore if
there are several numbers used in the same sentence, some of
which would normally be written out and some written as
figures, it is essential that *all be written as figures:* "The 28,145
Italians, the 900 Greeks, the 68 Spaniards, and the 1,456 Chinese
were . . ." This practice may even be extended to whole
paragraphs or pages of text, provided that there are enough

17. Frequently four digit numbers are written without the comma. This
usage is often preferred in numbers like 1100 and 3500, which the reader
pronounces to himself eleven hundred and thirty-five hundred. *Never use
commas in a four-digit date:* 1941; never 1,941.

numbers to justify it. Numbers preceding "per cent" should not be written out even when used in the text: 12 per cent. Notice that the per cent sign, %, is not used in the text, but may be used in the notes. Do *not* start a sentence with a figure; spell it out or rearrange the sentence.

## D. DATES

When your mention of a date is designed merely to set an event in time use the form, January 1, 1914, or 16 January 1914. Do not use January first, or 16th, or sixteenth. However if you are talking about January twenty-third as an event this written-out form is entirely proper. "January twenty-third was a bad day from beginning to end." The dates within the month are always written as cardinal numbers and are never spelled out. This holds always for both text and notes. Names of days and months, on the other hand, should always be written out in full when they appear in the text. They may be abbreviated in the footnotes.

If you are writing of the events of a month and are not concerned with the day write January 1941, without the comma between month and year.

In the expression: 1856–67, note that the century designation is left off the second date. As I have noted before, never *repeat* a century's number. However, when the span of years you are citing turns a century, naturally it is essential that you write out both years in full: 1895–1906, 1895–1900.[18]

Decades may be written in the following forms: the 90s, the Nineties, the 1890's, the 'nineties. The last is preferred usage.

Indicate the alternative years of the old and new calendar (O.S. and N.S.) with a slant line: 1776/77. Do *not* use the hyphen or dash.

18. Notice the form: He was in office from 1860 to 1866. To write this: "He was in office from 1860–1866," or "from 1860 to 66" or from "1860–'66," is distinctly wrong.

## E. Titles

Always in every instance write out "President," "Senator," "Congressman," "Secretary" (when referring to a cabinet officer), "Governor," "Professor." Do not abbreviate them. Write out "the Reverend" and "the Honorable" wherever space will permit. (Note that "the Reverend" and "the Honorable" must be used with a first name, initials, or another title: the Reverend John Jones, or the Reverend J. S. Jones, or the Reverend Dr. Jones. Never: the Reverend Jones.)

Write out all other titles if used with the last name: Captain Barker, Major General Smith. But these titles are abbreviated when used with a first name or initials: Capt. B. F. Barker, Maj. Gen. John Smith.

## F. Spelling

Modernize all spelling in quoted passages. Do not reproduce abbreviations in the out-of-date forms which demand that certain letters be written in tiny type and raised a half space above the rest of the line. Whatever you do, do *not* write "ye" for "the." The thing that looks like a "y" was originally a double letter called a thorn and was pronounced as "th" from the beginning.

Webster's dictionaries should settle all matters of modern spelling.

## G. Punctuation

The formal rules of punctuation are virtually endless. One may read them in any book on rhetoric or usage [19] and gasp. Happily modern writers are not much impressed by them, and tend to punctuate primarily to serve the ends of clarity. Today's trend is very definitely away from overpunctuation.

19. See for example, *Chicago Style Book*, pp. 78–112; or Paul N. Landis, *Freshman Composition* (Boston, 1940), pp. 242–263.

## 1. Comma

Use the comma after each of the words or phrases in a series of three or more: George, Henry, and John; the arduousness of collecting, the painfulness of criticizing, and the pleasure of scrapping. Use the comma (ordinarily) before clauses introduced by conjunctions such as: "and," "but," "for," "or, "nor," if a change of subject takes place: The system of Newtonian physics which swept over the west was an epochal one, and its results upon the current concept of life were tremendous. No comma is necessary when this sort of sentence is short: John hit Mary and Mary began to bawl.

## 2. Semicolon

Use the semicolon to separate two independent clauses, either one of which might stand as a sentence: He pulled the trigger; the hammer dropped with a harmless click; the gun was not loaded. Use the semicolon to separate long clauses which have commas within them: This is a grave matter in morals, faith, and ethics; indeed, it may be thought of as concerning the cosmos itself.

## 3. Colon

Use the colon to separate a grammatically complete clause from a second one that contains an illustration or amplification of its meaning: [20] Feverishly he began the study of palmistry: the phony science helped him not a bit. Use the colon instead of the words "namely," "to wit," "as follows," "for example," or similar expressions: Many of the group had very decided views: Brown was for open annexation; Smith, for a hands-off policy. Use the colon to introduce a formal statement, an extract, a speech in dialogue: We quote from the address: "Friends, Romans, Countrymen! . . ." Use the colon to indicate the sub-

20. *Chicago Style Book* § 138.

title of a book: *France: A Nation of Patriots; Germans in the Cameroons, 1884–1914: A Case Study in Modern Imperialism.* It is understood that what follows the colon is the subtitle.

### 4. Dash

Use the dash sparingly. It may be used effectively in place of parentheses from time to time; it may also be used in place of commas to set off a phrase in apposition: The man injured his elbow—at least this was his contention—and promptly brought suit. Hawks and owls—birds of prey—are carnivors; but strangely enough, are more easily tamed than the larks and sparrows.

### 5. Period

Use the period after the abbreviated titles "Dr." "Mr." "M." etc. But omit the period after "Mme" and "Mlle," "St" and "Ste" in conformity with French usage. Omit period after Roman numerals in titles: Henry IV, Pius IX, etc.

### 6. Ellipsis

Indicate omissions from a quotation by *three* dots—not two, or four, or five—*three* of them. Necessary punctuation must always be given in addition, and its correct spacing is a very important and difficult matter. Because there has been so much confusion on the matter the following rather full explanation is offered. Consider the following passage:

Carpenters, tanners, coopers, fullers, weavers, and all other artisans were welcomed in the settlement. Nor did the elders place any obstruction in the way of transient day laborers so long as these men behaved themselves. The rigid discipline of the community soon impressed itself upon the least God-fearing, and those who stayed to work, stayed also to pray. The master's order, "to prayer or damnation, ye miscreants!" found ready ears.

Now to cut and demonstrate various uses of the ellipsis symbol.

First example: "Carpenters, tanners, . . . and all other artisans were welcomed in the settlement. . . ." (Notice the comma after "tanners." Notice also the four dots after "settlement." The first of these is the period closing the sentence, and it must be placed as close to the word as it would be if there were no ellipsis. The succeeding three are the symbol of something left out.)

Second example: "Carpenters, . . . and all other artisans were welcomed . . ." (Notice that since the sentence does not end with "welcomed" only three dots are required.)

Third example: "The master's order 'to prayer . . . !' found ready ears." (Notice that the exclamation point is preserved at the end of the quoted passage. It is kept in only because the sentence is resumed. If this sentence were bitten off at the word "prayer" the exclamation point would disappear.) "The master's order 'to prayer . . .'" was always heeded.

## 7. Parentheses

There is a strong tendency away from using parentheses in the text as a locked cupboard for phrases in apposition. If such phrases must be set apart, commas, or, if a stronger device is required, dashes, are considered preferable: The man—the one wearing the galoshes—is the one who did it. Note: When parentheses are used no punctuation ever precedes the first parenthesis.

## 8. Square Brackets

Words interpolated into a quotation by yourself or by any person exercising an editorial function are enclosed in square brackets: "Carpenters, . . . all other artisans . . . [and even] transient day laborers . . ." They are also used to enclose the

word "sic" (see p. 96) or to set apart *your correction* of a mis-
spelling or obvious misstatement in a quotation: "Carpters
[sic] . . ." or "Carpters [Carpenters] . . ."

## 9. Quotations

Place within the closing quotation marks punctuation which
is part of the quotation; place outside the marks punctuation
which is part of your sentence. Example: Jackson proposed the
toast, "Our Federal Union; it must be preserved!" Could anyone doubt that this was challenge to Calhoun, "the ambitious
Demagogue"? But note that for sake of appearance many
modern presses always place the comma and period inside the
closing quotation marks instead of outside, regardless of the
punctuation of the original quotation. This is permissible
practice.

Passages of about seven typed lines and longer should be
quoted as follows: Leave a blank line between the last line of
your text and the first of the quotation. *Without any quotation
marks* begin the quotation at the left-hand margin. Do *not* indent. Type the quotation in single-space. End it *without quotation marks*. Skip a line and resume your double-spaced text
at the left-hand margin. Passages shorter than seven lines may
be handled this way if they occur on the same page as the
longer one. If the next sentence of your text is the first of a new
paragraph, naturally, indent it.

When one of these longer quotations is set up in type, the
printer will use a slightly smaller type face.

*Warning.* If a passage is not quoted from a source, but is
quoted from a book which claims to quote it from the source, do
*not* give the source reference without careful checking. If the
source is not available for checking, use the following device in
the note: 1. *Le National*, 27 July 1830, requoted from Allison,

*Thiers and the Monarchy*, p. 112. Be careful to make these citations accurate as to capitalization, punctuation, and spelling.

## H. LATINISMS

To the pedantic tradition belong the obscurities of abbreviated Latin. When this school means "see above" it writes "*vide supra*"; when it means "and following," [21] it writes "*et seq.*"; when "compare," it writes "cf." There is little excuse for using such phrases so long as suitable English equivalents exist.

There are however Latinisms which have become part of our language and they, of course, may be used with impunity: "i.e.," "e.g.," "viz.," and the like. There are also Latin words, which, though still unnaturalized, are exceedingly useful: "*ibid.*," "*passim*," "*sic.*"

"*Ibid.*," [22] which means "in the same place," is used in a footnote as a substitute for an author's name and the title of the work. It may be so used only when reference is to the same work as the last previous citation of your paper. For example:

1. *Chicago Style Book*, p. 5.
2. *Ibid.*, p. 26. (This means *Chicago Style Book*, p. 26.)
3. *Yale Style Book*, p. 75.
4. *Chicago Style Book*, p. 80; *Yale Style Book*, p. 18.
5. *Ibid.*, p. 23. (This means *Yale Style Book*, p. 23, only.)

As may be seen in the example, any intervening footnote material (except quotation or commentary) prevents the use of "*ibid.*" until the title has been repeated. "*Ibid.*" is always capitalized at the beginning of a note or sentence, and is always written in italics.

"*Passim*" means "throughout." It is used in a note in place of a multitude of page references. For example: If an author has

---

21. "and following" is frequently abbreviated "ff."
22. There are some very subtle and quite confusing distinctions between *ibid.* and *idem*. For simplicity's sake let's forget about *idem*.

developed a thesis in the course of three chapters of his book, and you do not wish to note every page in which he makes salient points, you may use *"passim"* thus: 1. S. B. Fay, *World War*, I, chaps. I-III *passim*. It is always italicized.

*"Sic"* means "thus." It is used in text and notes to indicate that a peculiarity in a quoted passage is the work of the original writer and not that of the quoter. Thus: He said, "He wouldn't do busness [*sic*] with him." It should be clearly understood that *"sic"* is justifiable only where some ambiguity might arise in its absence. For example, there would be no sense in using it after a quotation which was manifestly archaic or illiterate throughout. But where an otherwise careful and literate writer makes an obvious mistake in fact or spelling, or uses an expression in a misleading way, it is entirely proper for the quoter to show that he is aware of the error and that it is not his.

## I. Italics

Italics are represented in typescript by underscoring. They should be used as follows:

### 1. Emphasis

A writer whose most important thought hangs on the understanding of a single word or phrase, may italicize it. Beware of too much italicizing for emphasis; remember about crying "wolf, wolf" for fun. There will come occasions when a common word like "bureau" or "lattice" or "head" is used in a highly technical sense. Unless the reader knows of this rare usage he may get confused. Italic type is the best way to warn him, yet too much italicizing is not desirable. An excellent way around the difficulty is the following: Italicize the word when you mention it in your first definition or explanation. Possibly italicize it in your second use, then forget about the italics.

If the author wishes to italicize within a quoted passage, he should claim the italics as his own, thus: "He stoutly maintained that Russia *alone* [italics mine] [23] was responsible for the last war."

## 2. Book Titles

See above, p. 67.

## 3. Foreign Words and Expressions

Foreign words and expressions that are not accepted in English should be italicized: "*Bitte,*" he said; a *pis aller;* but not spaghetti, chauffeur, or sauerkraut; nor per se, a priori, a posteriori, a fortiori.

# V. PREFACE

The preface is the place where the author speaks *personally* to the reader. He tells how he happened to write the book, what other books in the field already exist and why he wants to refute or revise their conclusions. He describes how his book is composed and roughly outlines the thesis which he hopes to establish. The preface is also the place where the author pays his respects to the people who helped him with his book, thanks his benefactors, mentions the foundations under which he has worked. It is the place where he stays out of jail by making the proper acknowledgments to publishers whose books he has been quoting.[24] It is the place where he pays a tribute to the little woman "without whose aid this book . . ." If he's going to be funny, here's his chance. And unless he is Bernard Shaw he ought to be brief.

23. Or this may be put in a footnote, thus: Italics mine.
24. These permissions are necessary only when the essay or book is going to be published. Authors should be careful about them.

## VI. INTRODUCTION

The introduction, on the other hand, is the author's first *professional* encounter with the reader. It is the place where he attempts to lead the reader from his peaceful homelife into the general field of the essay. Carefully and clearly he sets the subject in time and place and milieu; he tries to give the reader a feeling of security by relating his small specific topic to the larger world of generally known fact. He tries to attach it to those things any well-informed reader already knows. Oftentimes the introduction is the first chapter of the book and is listed in the table of contents as Chapter I, Introduction.

Few parts of the author's work are of more importance, for if the introduction is badly done most readers will not advance beyond it. Accordingly it should be as gladdening and as enspiriting as the heavy-burdened scholar can contrive; it should carry the feeling: "This is exactly the book you've always wanted to read on this subject."

## VII. APPENDIXES

Appendixes are overgrown footnotes. They contain material which is relevant to a part of the text, but which is too long to put in fine print at the bottom of the page. The material may be a long and unpublished document, a reasoned discourse on a controversial point, or a statistical table.

## VIII. INDEX [25]

See the Appendix.

25. Undergraduate essays in typescript *of course* need no index.

# IX. THE BIBLIOGRAPHICAL NOTE [26]

No essay of any academic pretensions whatever is complete without a bibliography. Today's scholars are happily veering away from the old practice of uncritically listing all the books they consulted for a given project. More and more are they using the "note" as the proper vehicle for bibliographical information. This is praiseworthy. The note, besides being infinitely more useful than the barren alphabetized book list, is more pleasant and informing both to write and to read.

In essence this bibliographical note is a short critical essay about the materials which the author has used in writing his study. Authors' names, book titles, publication dates, and so on, are all incorporated into running sentences.

Arrangement of the material within a note, or any sort of bibliography for that matter, ought to follow one general pattern. Within this large scheme personal preferences, and the peculiar demands of the material will make the detail of every note different from the last. The general pattern is simple. Every note should be made up of at least two (and sometimes three) main sections. The first of these (when it is used) is apt to be the shortest, for it is the one which deals with bibliographical aids. That is, it starts with a discussion of bibliographies and bibliographical articles and essays which cover the literature of the topic. For example, if the essay dealt with a subject from the Stuart period of English history the first entry in the first section of the note would be: Godfrey Davies, *Bibliography of British History: Stuart Period* (Oxford, 1928).[27]

The second section is the most important for it is here that the author discusses his sources. He should describe them in the order of their weight and their closeness to what he believes

26. Undergraduate essays must have bibliographies and, preferably, bibliographical notes.
27. See n. 6 of this chapter.

the truth. His description should consider the form of the materials—whether printed or manuscript—where they are to be found, the state of their preservation, their completeness, how they are sorted, indexed, catalogued, or calendared. In the last analysis it is the topic of the essay which determines what is and what is not source material. If the essay is in the field of straight political history the sources may be arranged in this general pattern:

I. Manuscripts [28]
    A. Documents of state (archival)
    B. Documents of state (in private collections)
    C. Private documents
       1. Diaries, correspondence, unpublished memoirs
II. Printed Materials
    A. Documents of state (printed)
       1. Reports of commissions, parliamentary debates
    B. Private documents
       1. Published diaries, memoirs, letters

But if the subject under investigation is from intellectual history, the sources might be diametrically different. For example, if the essay were *The History of the Writing of Text-books in English History*—the source material would be the textbooks themselves. Hence any attempt to outline a formal method of listing and describing the sources in a bibliographical note is hopeless. The one encompassing rule is this: enter first the materials which are, in your judgment, the closest to the fact, the ones which the past has most unconsciously passed on for your use; enter next the ones which lie less close to the fact, the ones which have passed through the hands and minds and personalities of some intermediary. Thus in political history, manuscripts come before printed stuff because they have not gone through an editor and a printer. Printed documents of state come before the printed correspondence of private in-

28. Citation of manuscripts in the bibliography follows the same form as the first citation in a footnote. See pp. 75–77 in this chapter.

dividuals, because it is commonly believed that they are more impersonally gotten out. By the same token, the textbooks of the other topic would come before the comment upon them, even if the comment was contemporaneous.

The third section comprises the so-called secondary literature; it should contain all material which cannot be positively identified as source stuff. It too should be subdivided into at least two subclasses: monographs and general works. If newspapers and journals of opinion, autobiographies, memoirs, and diaries have been used and if they are not classable as sources, they should come in this section in their own subclasses.

Nearly all of today's historical writing ends with a bibliographical note such as the one being described. Students should be sure to look up a few of them and see how they are put together. The volumes in the Langer [29] series and in the Schlesinger and Fox series [30] can stand as models. See also the recent volumes in the Yale and Harvard Historical Series.

The note which follows is something of a hybrid. Because this book was not written from the sources and made no pretense at originality, there seemed to be little reason to follow the rules just laid down. For this reason the note will make a very poor model for student essay writers. About its only usefulness, beyond its content, is the manner in which the technique is demonstrated. The running comment which envelops author's names, titles, dates of publication, and so on, it is hoped, will illustrate some of the points made a few pages back.

29. W. L. Langer, ed., *The Rise of Modern Europe.*
30. A. M. Schlesinger and D. R. Fox, eds., *A History of American Life.*

# Bibliographical Note

Although nearly everyone knows that there is a huge number of volumes of history about this or that event, not so many realize that there is an unbelievably large literature about the subject, history, itself. The following bibliography, which is a very close selection of some of the most readable and helpful books, aims to do no more than generally introduce history—not in the sense of memory of things said and done—but in the sense of an experience, a literature (comparable to drama or poetry), a philosophy, and a method of unraveling truth. Everyone who has been through the effort of writing a serious historical essay should get a great deal of pleasure from reading into the history of history.

## I. Bibliographical

The bibliography at the end of the article by Henri Berr and Lucien Fabvre, "History and Historiography" in the *Encyclopedia of the Social Sciences* (15 vols. in 7, N.Y., 1937) is one of the completest and most up-to-date. There are other good bibliographical notes accompanying F. J. C. Hearnshaw's article, "The Science of History," in William Rose, ed., *An Outline of Modern Knowledge* (N.Y., 1931), pp. 773–811; and Harry Elmer Barnes' article "History," in the *Encyclopedia Americana* (N.Y. and Chicago, 1922), XIV, 205–264.

## II. Introductory

Wallace Notestein, "History" in, no ed., *On Going to College* (N.Y., 1938) is a thoughtful and charming essay on what a student may expect to get from the study of history. James Harvey Robinson, "History," in *Columbia University: Lectures on Science, Philosophy, and Art* (N.Y., 1907–08) gives a wise and measured review of the study of history and its large problems. Joseph W. Swain, "What Is History?" *Journal of Philosophy*, XX (1923), 281–289, 312–327, 337–349, is an excellent introduction to the philosophical interpretation of history. One of the very best books on the subject ever done is Charles Harold Williams, *The Modern Historian* (London, 1938). Here the author contrives to touch upon every phase of history and practically every one of its problems by quoting short passages from the words of the great historians themselves. Lucy M. Salmon's *Why Is History Rewritten* (N.Y., 1929), is a compelling and certainly not-too-difficult discussion of the subjective qualities of written history. Gaetano Salvemini's *Historian and Scientist* (Cambridge, Mass., 1939) goes over the differences between history and natural science with a delightful freshness of humanity and wisdom. Henry C. M. Lambert, *The Nature of History* (Oxford, 1933) is another excellent general summary. E. E. Kellet, *Aspects of History* (London, 1938) discusses history as theology, literature, science, propaganda, art and science, ethics, and economics.

Allan Nevins, *The Gateway to History* (Boston and N.Y., 1938) discusses what might be called the externals of historical study: the raw materials of the historian, the problems which confront him, the methods he uses to attack these problems.

## III. Philosophical

Raymond Aron, *Introduction à la philosophie de l'histoire* [Paris, 1938] though certainly not an easy book, is nevertheless an admirable introduction to the general field of the philosophy of history. The author gratifyingly assumes an ignorance on the part of the reader and endeavors to lead him gently into the abstrusities of the subject. Less profound and also exceedingly helpful is Henri Sée, *Science et philosophie de l'histoire* (2nd rev. ed., Paris, 1933).

The best introduction in English to the epistemology of written history is Maurice Mandelbaum, *The Problem of Historical Knowledge* (N.Y., 1938). In the admirable first part of the book, he rehearses the arguments of the *Relativist* school (those who claim that there is no absolute historical truth), discusses the principles of three important members of this school—Croce, Dilthey, and Mannheim—and the work of four *non-Relativists* (those who claim that historical truth is ascertainable)—Simmel, Rickert, Scheler, and Troeltsch. The second part of the volume represents his own astute but not entirely convincing argument on the side of absolute historical knowledge. The bibliographical information in the notes and bibliography itself is a very fine critical selection of the best work in the large area of the philosophy of history.

At a less technical, though no less worthy level, Carl L. Becker, "Everyman his Own Historian," in a book of essays bearing this title (N.Y., 1935) and Charles Beard, "Written History as an Act of Faith," *American Historical Review,* vol. 39 (1933–34), 220–231; and "That Noble Dream," *American Historical Review,* vol. 41 (1935–36), 74–87, write for the side of relativism. Charles H. McIlwain's "The Historian's Part in a Changing World," *American Historical Review,* vol. 42 (1937–38), 207–224, is one of the ablest replies in English.

## IV. The History of Historical Writing

Two useful but by no means perfect works by Harry Elmer Barnes, *A History of Historical Writing* (Norman, Okla., 1937), and the long article "History" which appears in the *Encyclopedia Americana* may serve as introductions into the general subject. Their value lies in the immense amount of factual and bibliographical information they contain. Robert

Flint's two volumes, the "France" sections of which overlap one another, *The Philosophy of History in France and Germany* (London, 1874), and *Historical Philosophy in France, French Belgium, and Switzerland* (N.Y., 1894) which supersedes it, are somewhat out-of-date, but nevertheless very useful and informing books. Be it said that the latter volume contains almost two hundred pages of comment on the earliest western historians; the next five hundred pages deal with France; and only the last short chapter touches Belgium and Switzerland.

The earliest historical writing (from the first written word through St. Augustine) is well covered in James T. Shotwell, *The History of History* (rev. ed., N.Y., 1939). Bibliographical suggestions throughout the book are suggestive of a large literature. The historians of the Old and New Testaments, the famous Greeks and Romans are ably discussed. On the greatest of the Greeks—Herodotus, Thucydides, and Polybius, J. B. Bury, *The Ancient Greek Historians* (N.Y., 1909) is still the classic.

There is no single work devoted to the historians who lived in the Medieval period. Barnes' work (see p. 105 of this note) gives adequate bibliographical suggestion for the important ones, and the "history" chapters of A. W. Ward and A. R. Waller, eds., *The Cambridge History of English Literature* (14 vols. and 1 index vol., Cambridge, Eng., 1907–33) are generally good for the early English chroniclers and annalists.

There is much the same gap in the historiography of the Renaissance. Here again one must call upon Barnes for directions. So also may one consult the far greater work of Eduard Fueter, *Geschichte der neueren Historiographie* (3rd ed., Munich, 1936). Emile Jeanmaire has made a French translation of the first edition which appears under the title: *Histoire de l'historiographie moderne* (Paris, 1914). Fueter may safely be considered the best guide for most historiographical problems in all the ages which follow the Renaissance.

The best introduction to the historiography of the Reformation is Franz Schnabel, *Deutschlands geschichtliche Quellen und Darstellungen in der Neuzeit, I: Das Zeitalter der Reformation, 1500–1550* (Leipzig and Berlin, 1931).

Preserved Smith in *A History of Modern Culture* (2 vols., N.Y., 1930–34), I, 252–278; II, 226–259, gives a general discussion of historical writing between the Reformation and the French Revolution. With a short amount of space dedicated to each man, Smith moves through a rapid consideration of the great and less great historians of his period. Sleidan, Bodin, Sarpi, Voss, Clarendon, and Bossuet; and, in the later century, Burnet, Mabillon, Vico, Bolingbroke, Turgot, Voltaire, Hume, Robertson, and Gibbon are a few of the best headliners. It should also be noted that a number of other men whose reputations are not primarily those of the historian, but who are important in any historiographical study, appear in other chapters of the book. The bibliographical information in the two notes (I, 629–630; II, 660–661) is enough to open this whole field up to the student who wishes to go farther.

John Bennet Black's *The Art of History: A Study of Four Great Historians of the Eighteenth Century* (London, 1926) devoted to Voltaire, Robertson, Hume, and Gibbon, is an excellent critical evaluation of the work of these great men, and, by intent, a study of the modes of written history in the eighteenth century.

The outstanding work on the last century is George P. Gooch, *History and Historians in the Nineteenth Century* (2nd rev. ed., London and N.Y., 1913). Covering the whole vast field of European and American historical writing, it is an interesting, helpful, and acute study. It is a perhaps unnecessary unkindness to say that a new edition, which would incorporate recent information and interpretations, is in serious demand. But no matter how far out-of-date, the book is still the best of its kind in English.

The following are some outstanding contributions to descriptive historiography which have appeared since Gooch. The only single volume work on the historiography of the United States is that of Michael Kraus, *A History of American History* (N.Y., 1937). As a general survey it is adequate and useful, but more acute evaluations of our great historians may be found in other studies which do not attempt its breadth. For example, William T. Hutchinson, ed., *The Marcus W. Jernegan Essays in American Historiography* (Chicago, 1937) is a collection of essays on the great Americans of yesterday by many of the eminent Americans of today. The two books: John Franklin Jameson's *The History of Historical Writing in America* (Boston and N.Y., 1891), which is still an admirable appreciation of the trail-breakers in American historiography; and John Spencer Bassett's *The Middle Group of American Historians* (N.Y., 1917) together furnish an excellent general orientation. William B. Trent and others, eds., *The Cambridge History of American Literature* (4 vols., N.Y., 1917–21) contains very good chapters on the historians of the United States. John Spencer Bassett, "The Present State of History Writing," in Jean Jules Jusserand and others, *The Writing of History* (N.Y., 1926) is a good short summary of American historiography. Walton E. Bean, "Revolt among the Historians," *Sewanee Review*, vol. 47 (1939), 330–341, is a penetrating analysis of the currents in American historiography since the founding of the American Historical Association in 1884. Most of his material is from the presidential addresses read at the annual meetings. W. Stull Holt, "The Idea of Scientific History in America," *Journal of the History of Ideas*, I (1940), 352–362, interestingly reviews what the science boom in the nineteenth century did to historical studies, especially in the United States.

The Whig bias in the historical writing of some of the nineteenth-century English historians is splendidly reviewed in H. A. L. Fisher, "The Whig Historians," British Academy, *Proceedings*, XIV (1928), 297–339. Fisher writes with special reference to Macaulay and his kinsman Sir George Trevelyan.

The best book on historical writing in modern Germany is Georg von Below, *Die deutsche Geschichtschreibung von den Befreiungskriegen bis zu unsern Tagen* (Munich and Berlin, 1924). H. A. L. Fisher, "Modern German Historians" in *Studies in History and Politics* (Oxford, 1920) is a wise and sympathetic treatment of the great Germans of the nineteenth century.

Gooch himself wrote a postscript to his own words about the historians of the French Revolution. It appears as "The Study of the French Revolution" in his *Studies in Modern History* (London and N.Y., 1931). Crane Brinton's note in his *A Decade of Revolution* (N.Y., 1934), pp. 293–302, on these same historians is one of the very best historiographical comments ever written. Another very good essay on this subject is Louis R. Gottschalk's "The French Revolution: Conspiracy or Circumstance," in *Persecution and Liberty: Essays in Honor of George Lincoln Burr* (N.Y., 1931). This essay and Brinton's are in substantial agreement on the large issues, but by no means repeat one another.

Again G. P. Gooch filled a gap in his earlier work when he wrote *Recent Revelations of European Diplomacy* (4th rev. ed., London and N.Y., 1940). Here he discusses the recent historians of modern diplomatic history.

Anatole G. Mazour, *An Outline of Modern Russian Historiography* (Berkeley, 1939) is easily the best treatment in English. Heinrich Finke, "Das Aufblühen der Geschichtsforschung in Spanien," *Historische Zeitschrift*, vol. 113 (1914), 70–82, is an excellent survey of Spain's nineteenth-century contribution to history. A. Curtis Wilgus, *Histories and Historians of Hispanic America* (Washington, 1913) is more a bibliographical than historiographical essay. Benedetto Croce, *Storia della storiographia italiana del secolo decimonono* (2nd ed., 2 vols., Bari, 1930) is the standard work.

## V. Historical Method

For excellent bibliographies in the broad field of historical method and for competently selected lists of the most useful books of factual material see: Cecil B. Williams and Allan H. Stevenson, *A Research Manual* (N.Y., 1940), appendix A; Louis Kaplan, *Research Materials in the Social Sciences* (Madison, 1939); and William Rose, ed., *An Outline of Modern Knowledge* (N.Y., 1931).

Johann Gustav Droysen, *Historik*, was the first attempt to approach the problem of modern historical method systematically. Delivered as a series of lectures in the 'sixties it was put into book form after Droysen's death from the notes of his devoted students. A shorter version of the work, *Outline of the Principles of History*, can be read in the English translation of E. Benjamin Andrews (Boston, 1893). Ernst Bernheim, *Lehrbuch der historischen Methode und der Geschichtsphilosophie* (6th rev. ed., Leipzig, 1908; 1st ed. 1889) is an important introductory work on method for those who read German. But it has been largely superseded by: Wilhelm Bauer, *Einführung in das Studium Geschichte* (2nd rev. ed., Tübingen, 1928). While covering the theoretical side of historical method, this book also goes deeply into the purely mechanical aspects of research: how to solve problems of chronology, paleography, diplomatics, as well as how to deal with subtler critical problems. The enormous bibliographical equipment in the footnotes lists (without descriptive or critical comment) the best general and monographic work on every conceivable side of historical research and writing. Unfortunately for the American student, the large part of these references are in German and French.

Nine years after Bernheim, C. V. Langlois and Charles Seignobos published their *Introduction aux études historiques* (Paris, 1898; trans. into English by G. G. Berry; rev. ed., London and N.Y., 1925). Resembling Bernheim's work, the book describes with magnificent clarity and depth the nature of the historical process in its philosophical aspects. For American students who do not read German, this book is the first required reading.

In addition to these classics there are a score of shorter and easier studies which are extremely useful. Fred M. Fling, *Outline of Historical Method* (Lincoln, Neb., 1899) might almost be considered a brief paraphrase of Bernheim and Langlois and Seignobos. Hereford B. George, *Historical Evidence* (Oxford, 1909) is much like Fling. John M. Vincent, *Historical Research: An Outline of Theory and Practice* (N.Y., 1911) is very useful on the mechanical side. Charles G. Crump, *The Logic of History* (London, 1919), and *History and Historical Research* (London, 1928) are short and clear statements of methodological problems. Charles Johnson, *The Mechanical Processes of the Historian* (N.Y. and Toronto, 1922) is an admirable short pamphlet. Allen Johnson, *The Historian and Historical Evidence* (N.Y., 1926) is light, easy, and exceedingly interesting.

More difficult for the beginner and written at a fairly high level of abstractness are the two splendid books of Frederick J. Teggart, *Prolegomena to History* (Berkeley, 1916), and *The Processes of History* (New Haven, 1918).

# APPENDIX

# Making an Index[1]

I. General Rules
 A. Capitalization
 B. Proper names
 C. Concrete nouns
 D. Topics
 E. Institutions
 F. Simplifying main headings
 G. Footnote material
 H. Subheadings
 I. Page and volume numbers
 J. Persons

II. The Actual Process of Indexing
 A. Preliminary marking of page proof
 B. Paper slips
 C. Entries on the slips
 D. Insuring accuracy in reading longhand notes
 E. Arranging slips—preliminary I
 F. Cross-referencing ideas
 G. Arranging slips—preliminary II
 H. Alphabetizing

1. This section on indexing, I can hardly claim. Nearly all of it comes from the kind help of three friends who have had more than their share of indexing difficulties. Leonard Labaree, Hartley Simpson, and Dorothy Gray I wish to thank from the bottom of my heart. I also wish to exonerate them for shortcomings which are likely to appear. With the ripeness of their experience they would have wisely hesitated before printing their advice. The shortcomings will be mine; I rushed in.

    I. Arranging slips—final
    J. Typing instructions
    K. Checking for errors
    L. Correcting page proof

III. Alphabetizing
    A. General
    B. Main heads
    C. Proper names
       1. M', Mc, and Mac; St. and Ste.
       2. Umlaut
       3. Spanish alphabet
       4. Compound names
       5. Names with a prefix
    D. Nouns and adjectives
    E. Book titles
    F. Numerals
    G. Abbreviations

IV. Sample

There is a nice story and a true one about the elderly Mommsen who received on his sixtieth birthday a *Festschrift* volume from his devoted students and friends. The old man rose and thanked the company, and as he sat down he rapidly noted that the fat work he held in his hand lacked an index. Audibly and with more vehemence than grace he was heard to say, "Dies ist wahrlich ein Cyclop." (*This is truly a lop-sided monster.*) And it was. Finished workmanlike books have indexes and good ones.

Most often the person using an index in a scholarly book goes to it with a specific problem in mind; he hopes to discover in the shortest possible time whether this particular book will give him the answer. Sometimes the problem is very simple: Does this author give any information about Lenin, or Themistocles, or Aimee MacPherson? Does he give any work on Berlin, Samarkand, or Winnemucca, Nevada? Sometimes it is very subtle and complicated indeed. Does this author consider British opinion on Turkey in terms of the Peace of Amiens? Does he take up seventeenth-century mercantilism in the light of present-day autarchy? The author, generally speaking, is almost the only person who knows the book well enough to foresee such questions and is, therefore, by definition the best man to make the index. This difficult and exasperating job is his final and profoundest obligation to the reader. He should realize that it is a difficult task and one *which will take him longer to do than he plans.* This is a warning.

Perhaps the most difficult feat the author must perform is changing himself at a few moments' notice from poised creator into uncertain, inquiring reader. But in order to make a satisfactory index, this transmigration of personalities must take place. Furthermore, the author must not imagine himself as a single reader; in a sense he must become all his readers. He must try to anticipate all of the questions which all of them will ask of his index. Plainly this is impossible. Nevertheless, the author can help almost every reader by contriving within the index an intelligent and imaginative system of cross references, and if after his heartbreaking labors, he succeeds in doing a good job, it will be one of the most useful and important parts of his work.

The following are general rules for making an index, and like other such rules will not fit all the oddities and peculiarities of every specific task. It is probable that the first person who tries to use them will encounter problems which defy them, or problems for which they give no answer. In this instance make up your own rules with your reader uppermost in mind, write them down and obey them consistently.

## I. GENERAL RULES

### A. CAPITALIZATION

Capitalize the first letter of every main heading.

## B. Proper Names

Index all proper names (persons and places) about which some information is actually given, omitting those which are only incidentally mentioned, or about which no true information is given.

Index the following under *Lenin*, but not under *Napoleon* or *Mars:*

> "Lenin, unlike Napoleon, achieved power without previously winning a reputation on the field of Mars."

Index the following under *San Francisco* and *Portland*, but not under *Mississippi:*

> "Important musical centers west of the Mississippi include San Francisco and Portland."

## C. Concrete Nouns

Index concrete nouns about which information is given which a reader is likely to seek.

Index the following under *Tobacco* and *Sugar* as well as under *Act of 1660* and *Enumerated commodities:*

> "The Act of 1660 included tobacco and sugar among the enumerated commodities."

## D. Topics

Index topics under such headings as will most probably occur to the reader searching for them. Here the indexer's ability to anticipate his reader's question is most significant. Example:

> "The contest between Blaine and Cleveland descended to about the lowest level of personal mud-slinging yet experienced in American political life. . . ."

Such a passage might well be indexed under *Election of 1884* (as well as under *Blaine* and *Cleveland*) even though the word *election* does not appear in the passage. It should be noticed that a passage must frequently be indexed under more than one topical head. A passage describing a letter from Jefferson Davis to General Lee on the conscription of Negroes should be indexed under the names of the *writer* and *recipient* and also probably under both *Conscription* and *Negro*.

## E. Institutions

Index institutions, etc., under either the first important word of their names or under the most important word, but be consistent in indexing parallel forms alike. Considerable cross referencing in such cases may be helpful. If, for example, you decide (as you should) to index *House of Commons* under *C* (Commons, House of) do not later index *House of Lords* under *H*. But cross reference to each under *House* may be desirable as also after all entries relating to *Parliament* in general (e.g. *See also Commons, House of; Lords, House of*).

## F. Simplifying Main Headings

You may find that a main heading becomes too fat and overladen with subheadings. If it begins to grow too complicated, the best remedy is to pick out some of the related subheadings and relegate them to a separate main heading of their own. For instance, in some books *Trade* would be too general a heading to carry all the subheadings that would come under it. *Free Trade*, if it had a substantial number of entries, could then be indexed under *Free Trade*, and cross-referenced from *Trade*. Or a number of major headings under *Trade* can be set up to relieve congestion, as:

Trade (containing all general references)
Trade, colonial
Trade, continental
Trade, domestic
Trade, treaties concerning

## G. Footnote Material

Authors and titles of works cited simply as authorities in footnotes should not be indexed. But proper names or subjects discussed in footnote commentary should be indexed when they would *not* be covered by the regular index entry from the text. That is, if the text were discussing Napoleon's brother Louis, and if a note from the word "Louis" discussed Hortense Beauharnais, his wife, and Louis Napoleon, his son, these two people should certainly appear in the index.

Material in footnotes should be designated by adding "n" to the page number on which the footnote *begins*, regardless of whether the note runs over one or more pages. Do not indicate the footnote number. Here is a more explicit illustration:

> [Text, p. 158] Franklin's keen interest in all contemporary forms of science is another illustration of the catholicity of his mind.[7]

> [Footnote] 7. His study of botany, for example, has only recently been investigated. See John Smith, *Franklin's Interest in Botany* (N.Y., 1936).

Index *text passage* under "Franklin, interest in science, 158" and "Science, Franklin's interest in, 158." Index *footnote passage* under "Botany, Franklin's study of, 158 n" but not under "Franklin" or "Smith."

## H. Subheadings

Indexes should include subheadings under each main heading. These subheadings should indicate briefly what the various page references are about. An index formed of headlines followed by groups of unexplained page numbers is not worth the time it takes to prepare. Whenever entries under the same main heading refer to different aspects of the general topic, they should be distinguished by appropriate subheads. (The only exception

comes when several of the references to a person are merely
casual—though not casual enough to be entirely excluded under Rule B above—when this occurs they may be grouped without subheads at the beginning of the main entry.)

Subheads should be brief but significant. Do not make them
abstracts of the whole textual statement, but so phrase them as
to indicate what the passage is *about*. They need not be worded
with grammatical relation to the main head, though sometimes
this is desirable. Definite and indefinite articles may usually be
omitted before nouns in subheads. Since the initial word of
the subhead is often a matter of convenience of wording rather
than of essential significance, subheads should be arranged under the main head *in the numerical order of their first page appearance* and not alphabetically. Under the same subhead may
be grouped all entries relating to the same aspect of the main
topic. Example:

> Smith, John (1834–85), 57, 192; birth, 126; marriage, 188–
> 189, 192; elected to Senate, 198 n; on agricultural prob-
> lem, 201, 226; supports administration, 213; attacked by
> Brown, 228 n; death, 238

## I. Page and Volume Numbers

Do not use p. or pp. in the index. Always write numbers out
in full. Thus: 23–35, 135–196; *not* 23–5, 135–96

If you are making a single index for several volumes, naturally
the volume as well as the page number must be given. Use
Roman numerals for volume numbers, and separate volume entries by semicolons. Thus: I, 15, 17, 19–25; II, 16–18; III,
260

If the reference is to material in a footnote, leave a space
between the number and the letter "n". Thus: 126–128, 136 n,
138

Separate numbers by a comma. Use a semicolon between
subheads.

Do not put a period after the last number of your entry. But put a period after an entry which is a cross reference. Thus:

> Adelbert, King of the Franks, 56–67, 68
> America, land of opportunity. *See* Opportunity, industrial.

Topics which run over two or more pages of the text should be indexed by inclusive page numbers wherever possible, rather than by one page number followed by "f" or "ff". The latter method tends to be unsatisfactorily vague.

### J. PERSONS

Whenever information can be obtained, persons listed in the index should be identified by first names or at least by initials. When there are two or more men of the same name they should be further identified by their dates. With officials, it is often desirable to indicate the position held, though this is not essential except when confusion might arise among two men of the same name.

When the text mentions a man by both family name and title, index him under his family name, and put his title in parenthesis. Enter the title in its correct alphabetical place and cross-reference to the family name. Thus:

> Beaconsfield, Earl of. *See* Disraeli, Benjamin.
> Disraeli, Benjamin. (Earl of Beaconfield), birth, 195

## II. THE ACTUAL PROCESS OF INDEXING

### A. PRELIMINARY MARKING OF PAGE PROOF

Some professional indexers first go through the entire page proofs underlining with one colored pencil all proper names to be indexed and, with another, key words to all topics and subjects to be listed. When you index your own work, this preliminary marking is not always necessary, although you should do some advance planning of the major topics which will be important heads.

## B. Paper Slips

Provide yourself with a considerable supply of slips of paper of uniform size. Slips 2″ x 3″ are adequate, though some indexers prefer 3″ x 5″. Cards are not necessary. They add to the bulk to be handled as well as the expense of the task.

## C. Entries on the Slips

Beginning with page 1, go through the page proofs carefully, page by page, making a separate slip for each entry. Make as many separate slips as there are to be entries of a given passage. Each slip should have at the top the main head, below this the appropriate subhead, and the page number. Illustration:

> "Governor Brown urged Senator Smith to support the pending tariff bill."

Slips should be: (1) Brown, Gov. William, urges support of tariff, 129 (2) Smith, Sen. Henry, urged to support tariff, 129 (3) Tariff, bill of 1832, support of urged, 129

## D. Insuring Accuracy in Reading Longhand Notes

It is assumed that the author will write out these entries in longhand and that when he comes to type out the slips, his own writing of proper names may mislead him. Many people's n's and u's, m's and w's, ch's and cl's are likely to resemble each other and to cause maddening errors in the typed and printed work. A useful trick is to make longhand n's of proper names like this: ñ; the u's like this: u̲; m's: m̄; w's: w̲; ch's: c̄h̄; and cl's: c̲l̲.

## E. Arranging Slips—Preliminary I

Do not try to arrange slips alphabetically as you go along, but place them in one pile. (At this point see paragraph K below on checking.) At convenient times (at the end of each chapter, say) it is well to sort the accumulated slips into twenty-six alphabetical piles, adding each to the similar group gathered from previous chapters or other sorting periods. As certain leading and frequently recurring main heads accumulate, it may be convenient to sort these out from the general group of that letter and hold as additional or subordinate groups to be later reincorporated in the proper places under that letter.

## F. Cross-Referencing Ideas

As you work along, ideas will suggest themselves for suitable cross references for the ultimate index. Whenever you think of such a desirable cross reference make a slip for it, adding it to the regular pile for ultimate sorting and inclusion.

## G. Arranging Slips—Preliminary II

When you have gone through the entire text (do not ordinarily index preface, appendix, or bibliography) and all slips have been sorted into twenty-six piles, the *A* pile should then be resorted and arranged alphabetically within itself. In this process all slips bearing the same *main head* will now come together. Among these, slips with the same *subhead* should be compared and page numbers transferred to the slip (with that subhead) having the lowest page number, and the other slips discarded. Frequently, such combinations can be made of entries bearing subheads which differ from each other only slightly. All slips bearing the same *main head* should now be arranged in ascending numerical order of the first page number on each slip.

## H. Alphabetizing

If the business of alphabetizing were a simple thing, here is where it would be included. It is not simple. It is treated as a separate entry, see pp. 124–130.

## I. Arranging Slips—Final

When all slips in the *A* group are thus sorted and arranged, proceed with the same process for the *B*, *C*, *D*, etc., groups. Some indexers prefer to type off each letter before final sorting of the next. The only objection is that in sorting a later letter some slips may be found which might more appropriately be included under a heading already typed.

## J. Typing Instructions

Type double-space across the whole page, beginning each main head with a capital letter and at the left-hand margin. Sub-heads (without capitals except in proper names) follow continuously on the same line or lines, indenting each overrun line three spaces. Leave two double-line spaces between the last entry of one letter and the first of the next. Cross references should be added as you go along and the whole resurveyed at the end for additional desirable cross references, and for possible transfers of entries to more suitable heads.

## K. Checking for Errors

When the whole index is typed it should be checked with the proof for errors. Theoretically, each entry should be looked up from the index, but this procedure is admittedly a counsel of perfection. If a thorough sampling here and there throughout discloses no appreciable errors, the entry-by-entry check may be dispensed with. A method which combines the maximum of check with the minimum of effort is as follows: After slips for a chapter have been made but before they have been sorted alphabetically (and are, consequently, still in one pile arranged numerically), check these back against the proofs of that chapter. If this is done chapter by chapter while preparing the slips, then at the end the completed index typescript need be checked only against the slips (now arranged alphabetically) instead of against the proofs.

### L. CORRECTING PAGE PROOF

In compiling index copy you have your last chance to detect proofreading errors and oversights. Watch out for them. In assembling slips inconsistencies of spelling proper names, etc., often become apparent for the first time. Correct them now on the page proofs. This is why it is desirable not to return page proofs to the printer until the index copy is prepared. Now is your last chance to make your book typographically perfect.

Remember that last-minute changes made in the text are likely to necessitate complementary changes in the index.

## III. ALPHABETIZING

Getting things in correct and consistent alphabetical order is more complicated than it seems at first glance. The following rules are recommended.

### A. GENERAL

Alphabetize through compound words, phrases, titles, etc., to the first comma.[2] Thus:

New, John S., 25
Newbury, town of, 171

2. But this is by no means a rigid rule, and many indexers prefer to index such entries as follows:

New, John S., 25
New England, people of, 68
New History, The, 156
New River, 115
Newbury, town of, 171
Newem, Gustav A., 59
Newfoundland, 190
News, 75–76
News items, foreign, 80
Newton, Mary, 96

Newem, Gustav A., 59
New England, people of, 68
New History, The, 156
News, 75–76
News items, foreign, 80
Newton, Mary, 96

## B. Main Heads

In arranging main heads alphabetically, if proper names or subject appear to be identical but refer to different persons or things, observe the following rules:

(a)  Person precedes place, place precedes subject.
(b)  Less fully identified persons precede those more fully identified,[3] the arrangement being alphabetical within each category. Illustration:

Castle, spy in British army          [Poorly identified person]
Castle, Colonel  ⎫                   [Partially identified persons al-
Castle, Miss     ⎭                     phabetically arranged]
Castle, Andrew   ⎫                   [Fully identified persons alpha-
Castle, T. J.    ⎭                     betically arranged]
Castle City, New Mexico              [Place]
Castle Guard                         [Subject]

3. The ordering of persons is however somewhat a matter of taste. It is quite as often done just the other way, with fully identified persons coming first, and the less fully identified persons trailing at the end. Under this arrangement, when there are several persons of identical Christian and surnames, titled persons come first, untitled after. Thus:

Howard, Charles, Earl of Nottingham
Howard, Sir Charles
Howard, Charles
Howard, [Charles ?]

## C. Proper Names

### 1. M', Mc, Mac; [4] St., Ste.

These are always listed as if they were spelled out—that is Mac, Saint or Sainte, etc.:

Mabelle
Mc Afee
MacDuff
Mackall
M'Kenzie
Macquaide
Macy

### 2. Umlaut

Always consider the umlauted vowel in German names as being a diphthong made up of the vowel and a following "e": Consider ä as ae, ö as oe, ü as ue. Examples:

| | |
|---|---|
| Adelbert | Oertel |
| Äbel | Öser |
| Affehaus | Offenbach |

Also realize that this rule holds for names in which the umlauted vowel is *not the first letter*. Examples:

4. Some indexers (including nearly all American library cataloguers) consider M', Mc, and Mac as a 27th letter in our alphabet; a letter which comes between "l" and "m." They therefore not only consider all the M', Mc, Mac forms as Mac, but also put them together in their own bracket. Thus:

Lvov

Mc Adam
M' Dill
Mac Flecknoe
Mac Levy

Mabelle
Macy

This usage is so widely employed that it may be considered equally valid and desirable.

Mabler
Mäller
Maföln
Mafogowitz
Moberg
Möbaum

### 3. Spanish Alphabet

The four letters of the Spanish alphabet which do not appear in ours: "ch," "ll," "ñ," and "rr," are indexed in Spanish works after the regular letters "c," "l," "n," and "r," respectively. American indexers can forget this practice (which if used would confuse most of their readers) so long as they remember to write ñ correctly.

### 4. Compound Names

Compound names whose parts are connected with an "and," "&," "y," "et," or "und," are listed under the first of the two names and alphabetized as if one continuous name. Examples:

Gilbert, Sir Humphrey
Gilbert y Martinez, Alfredo
Gilbert und Nebelhafl, Karl von
Gilbert and Sullivan, the Savoy Operas of
*Gilbert et Thomas*, Jean Pineau

Compound names whose parts are unconnected or hyphenated names are naturally listed under the first of the two names and alphabetized as if one name. Examples:

Larochefoucauld-Liancourt
Lionel-Smythe

### 5. Names with a Prefix

English and American names with a prefix should be listed under the prefix:

| | | |
|---|---|---|
| De Morgan | Van Buren | À Becket |
| De Vane | D'Israeli | La Farge |

French, Spanish, Italian, and Portuguese names are listed under the prefix *only* when the prefix is an article or a combination of an article and preposition:

| | | |
|---|---|---|
| La Follette | Del Monte | Du Deffand |
| Lo Gallo | Della Cruz | Di Sopo |

But if the prefix is a preposition alone or a separated preposition and article, you can list under either name or article: [5]

| | |
|---|---|
| Vinci, Leonardo da [6] | LaFontaine, de |
| La Cruz, de | Farina, da |

German, Dutch, and Flemish names are indexed under the name itself, *not the prefix.*

| | |
|---|---|
| Ribbentrop, von | Hoff, van't |
| Malen, van der | Husen, van |

Compounded names, of course, are always listed under the first letter.

| | |
|---|---|
| Macbride | Delacroix |
| Vanderbilt | Deliagre |

## D. Nouns and Adjectives

In general alphabetize under nouns and not adjectives: "organization, commercial"; *not* "commercial organization." But when the adjective is really part of a compound noun, alphabetize under the adjectival modifier: "South America"; *not* "America, South"; and "New Deal"; *not* "Deal, New." [7]

5. A too rigorous application of this rule is perhaps dangerous. A name like DeGaulle is so firmly fixed in the American mind as DeGaulle, that if indexed under Gaulle, de, it would remain unfound. On the other hand no French indexer would think of listing it in any form other than Gaulle, de. Perhaps the best way out of such a difficulty is to stick to the rule, and be generous with cross references: Under DeGaulle refer your reader to Gaulle, de.

6. This name too is of the sort which demands both a "d" and a "v" entry.

7. Like so many this rule is in general sound, but not absolutely to be followed. In certain types of books, one would look under *commercial or-*

## E. Book Titles

Book titles are always alphabetized under the first important word; articles and prepositions are ignored. Thus:

Washington, George
*The Way of All Flesh*, Samuel Butler
Wazir, mountaineers

*Science in Progress*, George A. Baitsell
*In the Spirit of Henry James*, Ralph B. Perry
Spoils system, description of

But it would be absurd to follow this rule to its end. Obviously, titles like *Among the Cannibals*, and *For Whom the Bell Tolls* should be listed in the "a's" and "f's" respectively; or at least be cross-indexed from these letters.

## F. Numerals

Main heads which begin with numerals should be listed as if the numbers were spelled out. Thus:

Eight, committee of
1897, class of *or*
Eighteen ninety-seven, class of
Erie railroad

---

*ganization* most naturally, and indeed it is questionable if anyone ever thinks to look under *organization* as a heading, unless a work has many passages that would come under that heading. But it is of course true that *New Deal* should be indexed under *New* and not under *Deal*. In the same way things like *Free Trade* present a problem. If *Free Trade* is an important subject in a work, it would be better to index it under *Free*, and then to cross-reference under *Trade*. Or if you found it necessary to have an entry *Geographical works*, there would not be much sense in putting it under *Works, geographical*. If a reader has geography on his mind, he turns to G in the index, not to W. Of course, the adjective-purist would say that the way out of that situation would be to index under *Geography, works on*, which is sensible. But you may find there are times when the adjective is the most efficient usage, as in *Proportional representation, Electoral College*. And there are certain adjectives which readers always like to find, such as *rural, industrial,* etc.

But if there are a number of dates from one century they should be arranged chronologically. Thus:

    1798, class of
    1858, class of
    1872, class of
    1896, class of
    1926, class of

The same rule holds for a list of kings or other titled persons who have the same name and for statutes which have the same general designation but are distinguished from one another by their numerals. Even if the numerals are spelled out these should not follow in alphabetical order. Thus:

| PEOPLE | STATUTES |
|---|---|
| Henry I | 7 Rich. II, c. 2 |
| Henry II | 1 Edw. IV, c. 1 |
| Henry III | 1 Edw. IV, c. 5 |
| Henry IV | 2 Edw. IV, c. 1 |
|  | 5 Chas. I, c. 15 |
| Nottingham, First Earl of | 10 Geo. I, c. 10 |
| Nottingham, Second Earl of | 2 Edw. VII, c. 6 |

## G. Abbreviations

Consider abbreviations as if they were the full word spelled out. Thus:

    Foster, Jack
    Foster, Jas. [provided this is the way in which James Foster
                  was referred to in the text]
    Foster, Janet

*A.H.R.*, if it has been used constantly in reference to the *American Historical Review;* or *P.M.L.A.* for *Publications of the Modern Language Association,* should be indexed under *American* and *Publications.* They should also be cross-referenced from *A.H.R.* and *P.M.L.A.*

## IV. SAMPLE

The following is a sample of a completed typescript of a fragment of an index. Note carefully the form and arrangement, punctuation, capitalization, methods of setting different kinds of cross references, etc. [*Superior figures used below are explanatory notes. A real index contains no footnotes.* In all other respects follow this sample exactly.]


Feudal incidents, loss of, through alienation, 135; liability for, 235–237; homage, 288–291, 301 (*see also* William I);[8] reliefs, 303, 588; marriage, *see* Wardship;[9] inquests on, 305, 357 n, 388. *See also* Escheat; Fealty; Services.[10]
Feudalism, decline of, 3–4, 129, 250–251; in Anglo-Saxon England, 10
Fines. *See* Scutage.[11]
Fish, William, tenant of Henry VII, 198 n
Fish, right to take in lord's pond, 245
Fisheries, monopoly of, 122
Fitz-Bernard, family of, 105. *See also* Jarponville, Albrega de.


Examples given in notes eight and nine occur only rarely. Ten and eleven are the common forms.

Hartley Simpson much of whose sage advice appears in the


8. Method of indicating cross reference to additional entries relating to a subhead. That is, besides pp. 288–291 and 301, references to *homage* as a feudal incident will also be found under the head of *William I*.

9. Method of indicating cross reference to *all* entries relating to a subhead. That is, all references to *marriage* as a feudal incident will be found under the head of *Wardship*.

10. Method of indicating cross reference to *additional* entries relating to a main head. That is, besides all entries here shown, additional references to *Feudal incidents* will be found under *Escheat, Fealty*, and *Services*.

11. Method of indicating cross reference to *all* entries relating to a main head. That is, all references to *Fines* will be found under the head of *Scutage*.

foregoing pages had a last comment in his memorandum to me. "One thing about indexing which everyone has omitted to say: The best place to do an index is in an insane asylum." Could it be that the editor of the Mommsen *Festschrift* . . . ?

# Index